THE
SPIRIT
OF WATER

INCLUDES PREVIOUSLY
UNPUBLISHED ICE CRYSTAL
PHOTOGRAPHS

LAWRENCE ELLYARD

First published by O Books, 2007
O Books is an imprint of John Hunt Publishing Ltd.,
The Bothy, Deershot Lodge, Park Lane, Ropley, Hants, SO24 OBE, UK
office1@o-books.net
www.o-books.net

Distribution in:

UK and Europe
Orca Book Services
orders@orcabookservices.co.uk
Tel: 01202 665432 Fax: 01202 666219 Int. code (44)

USA and Canada
NBN
custserv@nbnbooks.com
Tel: 1 800 462 6420 Fax: 1 800 338 4550

Australia and New Zealand
Brumby Books
sales@brumbybooks.com.au
Tel: 61 3 9761 5535 Fax: 61 3 9761 7095

Far East (offices in Singapore, Thailand, Hong Kong, Taiwan)
Pansing Distribution Pte Ltd
kemal@pansing.com
Tel: 65 6319 9939 Fax: 65 6462 5761

South Africa
Alternative Books
altbook@peterhyde.co.za
Tel: 021 447 5300 Fax: 021 447 1430

Printed in Singapore

THE
SPIRIT
OF WATER

INCLUDES PREVIOUSLY
UNPUBLISHED ICE CRYSTAL
PHOTOGRAPHS

LAWRENCE ELLYARD

Foreword by
Masaru Emoto
author of the New York Times bestseller
"The Hidden Messages in Water"

BOOKS

Winchester, UK
Washington, USA

Praise for the Spirit of Water

"The Spirit of Water is a must read for anyone interested in our mind's ability to influence one another and our environment. This is a timely message for all of us."

- Marci Shimoff, Co-author, *Chicken Soup for the Woman's Soul*, Featured speaker in the worldwide film phenomenon, *The Secret*

"A powerful book which teaches us the effect of positive thought on our material world. Nature becomes a sublime reflection, a mirror for our positive intent. This is a must read for those interested in helping to heal the world through consciousness."

Brandon Bays, author of *The Journey*

"The Spirit of Water is a beautiful proof of the interconnectedness of everything and from that, the profound influence each of us has".

- Gangaji, author of *The Diamond in your Pocket*

"The Spirit of Water provides a new-authentic perception of water. This book educates and delivers timely information which enhances the mind and body. A must read!"

- Gary Quinn, bestselling author of *Living In The Spiritual Zone*

"Water remains one of the most mysterious substances on planet earth. Because it is utterly necessary for life, it has been considered sacred by many spiritual traditions. Anyone wishing to penetrate the aesthetic, sacred, yet practical dimensions of water should read this book."

- Larry Dossey, MD, author of *The Extraordinary Healing Power of Ordinary Things*

"The Spirit of Water reminds us, with beauty, grace and admirable practical application, how important it is for us to be mindful of our thoughts, with their infinite power to influence even something as elemental as water."

- Noelle Nelson, Ph.D., author of *The Power of Appreciation: Key to a Vibrant Life*

"The Spirit of Water provides an excellent insight in to the subtle, beautiful and fascinating properties of water, something most of take for granted but which has the potential to greatly improve our physical, mental and spiritual well-being. Lawrence reveals the extraordinary properties of this pure, life-giving element and provides practical advice on how to access its healing and revitalising qualities."

- David Vennells, author of *The Healing Source Book.*

"Lawrence Ellyard has written a clear, readable introduction to a controversial topic. The material in this volume is of interest to a wide range of professional scientists and scholars as well as the layperson since it raises questions about the nature of reality and dovetails with challenging areas in consciousness research, quantum physics and parapsychology. It is recommended for those who want to read a well written account which invokes neither New Age hype nor mindless skepticism."

- Dr. Rafael Locke, National Director, Ikon Institute for Healing Arts and Sciences.

"It is said that water is the oil of the twenty-first century. Its supply is diminishing, yet it is necessary for the survival for life on this planet. This book describes many dimensions of this precious resource, some of them already known, such as the hazards of polluted water, and others still controversial, such as water's alleged "vibrational" properties... The latter section of the book presents many practical exercises to help readers attain a more balanced way of life, one in which their consumption of water's "life force" can be exemplified in their daily activities."

- Stanley Krippner, Ph.D. co-author, *Becoming Psychic*

"The Spirit of Water is a celebration of the qualities of water. Combining science, philosophy and traditional practical wisdoms including 'Hado' Lawrence Ellyard brings water alive for us. We are awakened to the fact that we are interconnected with water for not only our physical survival but for wellbeing on every level body, heart and soul. A fabulous and inspiring book!"

- Diane and Kerry Riley authors *Sexual Secrets for Men and Sexual Secrets for Women*

"Lawrence Ellyard's unusual book is definitely an eye-opener, in more senses than one. Too often we take water for granted. By exploring it intimately 'The Spirit of Water' should help increase our awareness of its true significance for us."

- Peter Lemesurier, author of The Gods Within

"The Spirit of Water is a fascinating exploration and development of the work started by Masaru Emoto. Lawrence Ellyard provides fascinating facts about water and its ability to record, store and transmit both positive and negative thoughts, actions and emotions. This book emphasises the importance of positive energy or hado in our every day lives in order to dispel negativity. Exercises are given to assist in bringing the mind, body and spirit back into balance and harmony. An excellent, down to earth, practical book that has something for everyone."

- Sue Allen, author of *Spirit Release - A Practical Handbook*

"The Spirit of Water unveils the sublime power of water and provides compelling views on how thoughts create structure; serving to unite the paths of science and Spirit. In this must read work, Lawrence Ellyard offers clear and essential practices for anyone interested in healing themselves and the environment."

- Laura Alden Kamm, author of *Intuitive Wellness*

"The Spirit of Water is a beautiful book that reminds us of how profoundly all things, even water, are affected by the energy around and within us. Filled with practical information, this book guides you to make good choices in the water you drink and the thoughts you think."

- Robin McKnight, M.A. author of *Change Your Reality, Change Your Life*

"The Spirit of Water blends scientific investigation with metaphysical concepts, producing an entertaining yet comprehensive discussion of the physical and spiritual properties of water. Lawrence Ellyard gifts us with priceless tools enabling direct communication with water thereby influencing its health and possibly rescuing our own in the process."

- Michelle Hanson author of *Ocean Oracle*

"It's been said that water will become the primary medicine of the 21st century. In The Spirit of Water, Lawrence Ellyard explains why this is so. Describing the amazing healing properties of properly balanced, positively energized water, and showing how anyone can "program" their water with conscious intent to purify, heal, and rejuvenate the cellular matrix of the human body, this book provides an excellent introduction to the nature of water and its vital role in health and healing."

- Daniel Reid author of *The Tao of Health, Sex, and Longevity* and *The Tao of Detox*

"The Spirit of Water explores the relationship we have with our 'mother substance' and illustrates the effect our thoughts and emotions have on the natural world - both in the physical sense and at a more subtle level. In his book, Lawrence Ellyard offers daily practices through which we can positively influence the energy present in water as well as utilize its life-giving force to enhance and enrich our life and the lives of those around us."

- Nancy Christie, author of *The Gifts of Change*

"Lawrence Ellyard gives us a clear understanding of the nature of water. It is sure to infuse every reader with appreciation and wonder for this most mysterious of our planet's resources. Read it and savour the knowledge he delivers so clearly and concisely."

- Katherine Gibson, author of *Pause: Putting the Brakes on a Runaway Life*

"My view of water has changed having read The Spirit of Water. The book demonstrates that what you project is what you will see, and what you see is what you project. Therefore, change must come from within."

- Julia Heywood, author *The Barefoot Indian*

"Lawrence Ellyard takes us on journey of self healing by way of deepening and evolving the ground-breaking ideas and perceptions about water originally brought to us by Masaru Emoto. This wonderful new book teaches us how to incorporate simple Hado principles into a daily spiritual discipline for enhancing lives, transforming communities and families, to heal our world."

- Susie Anthony, author of *A Map to God - Awakening Spiritual Integrity*

"The Spirit of Water is at the leading edge of current scientific controversy, with experimental verification of phenomena that demonstrate the presence of an all-pervading informing consciousness. Books of this kind are vital at this time as they provide a framework for the intellect to open up a dialogue with the soul."

- Altazar Rossiter, author of *Developing Spiritual Intelligence*

CONTENTS

This book is dedicated to my teacher
Masaru Emoto

FOREWORD BY MASARU EMOTO

It is with much pleasure that I write this foreword for Lawrence Ellyard's new book *The Spirit of Water*. Currently our world is in turmoil. It seems that many people are lost and are finding it difficult to know the way to the right direction. In times like this, I believe that we need to go back to the origin. And that origin is water, and therefore *hado*.

Hado is a term I have used to describe all the subtle energy that exists within the universe and therefore this includes ourselves. Through my research it became apparent to me that water improves or deteriorates depending upon the kind of information it takes in. We are also water, over 70 percent. The essence of a human being is water. It makes sense therefore that what we take in will either improve or deteriorate our health and wellbeing.

My twenty years of research is presented in a photography book called *Message from Water* and a second book called *The Hidden Message in Water*. These books have been embraced by millions of people around the world and today many people have created their own interpretation and philosophies around this work. Yet this message is still unknown to many people.

The author of this book, Lawrence Ellyard is a graduate of the International *Hado* Instructor School which I host. Lawrence is one of the first of my students that has caught on to my desire to train people who would spread the truth about the real form of water and the *hado* that is hidden within it.

Of course, what you will read in this book is not a copy of my thoughts but his original work drawing on his extensive background as a prominent natural therapist, teacher and author.

It is my hope that this book and its message will help bring you the positive energy life which is *hado*.

Masaru Emoto

Tokyo, Japan, November 2006

INTRODUCTION

What is the Spirit of Water? What hidden message does it carry for all of us? The answer lies in the emerging research of Masaru Emoto and his innovative discovery revealed through ice crystal photography. For over a decade, Masaru Emoto and the team at IHM in Tokyo, Japan (the International Health Medical Research Institute, established in 1986 by Masaru Emoto), have been photographing ice crystals from water that has been exposed to outer stimuli such as words, music, images and thoughts.

These images reveal how water stores and transmits information, revealing how our consciousness manifests through this liquid medium. This illustrates the ability of our minds to manifest consciousness in physical form. Ice crystal photography reveals a message for all of us, uniquely depicted in the stunning images presented within this book.

The essential message from water is that we are more powerful than we realize. What we do, say and even think has a dramatic effect upon water. After all, our bodies are mostly water (roughly 70 per cent). Imagine how our thoughts, words and actions affect our body. Our mind works the same way. Water is a mirror which reflects back to us the very nature of our mind. What Masaru Emoto was able to discover through his research is that everything has an underlying vibration. When water is exposed to outer stimuli it absorbs this information which is later observed under the microscope when frozen. Beautiful ice crystals form when exposed to positive vibration whereas a negative stimulus creates distorted formations. At the smallest sub-atomic level, everything is in a constant state of vibration. Ice crystal photography points to this.

The title of this book, *The Spirit of Water*, does not suggest that there are 'spirits' per say, in our water. Rather, it is that our consciousness or spirit can be imbued and carried by water. You might think of water much like an artist's canvas. Paint it with words, thoughts and actions and you will get a picture. The question is, what kind of pictures are we painting?

In our troubled world, Emoto's message is timely, perhaps now more than ever. That message is *"with our thoughts we create our world."* This message is nothing new. The sages throughout time have all taught this truth. What is new is that we can now observe this process in physical form and experiment with it. For many people their view is "I'll believe it when I see it." Through Masaru Emoto's images, 'seeing is now believing'. We co-create our world and it starts with each one of us. Can one person make a difference to themselves and our world through their thoughts and feelings? The answer is certainly yes.

In our modern times, water has lost its significance to many people. The sacredness of water was always acknowledged by ancient civilizations. They treated water as something sacred. It was revered and cherished as a divine substance of life and purity.

In today's world we have forgotten these things. Water is mostly neglected and seen as nothing more than a cheap commodity. Since water is fundamental to all life, valuing it properly will lead to valuing other things too – it is not possible to value water and not to value ourselves. Like a stone dropped into a still pond, the ripples touch every part of our being and ultimately our fragile world.

When we look upon the beauty of ice crystals, water is providing us an opportunity to see the world through a different lens. To thank water before we drink it and to feel gratitude for its life-giving properties is an attitude we all can share. It is from this place that we can once again honor water and likewise ourselves. It is this attitude of gratitude which can create an impetus for change.

Ice crystal photography reveals that we are so much more than our physical forms. What we experience in our daily lives is but the tip of an iceberg compared with the potential of our minds. Ice crystal photography reveals that the mind is an array of endless possibilities dancing in the free play of space. When we focus our minds, this unlimited potential concentrates into one place and can be imprinted in water.

Masaru Emoto's work shows us a way to measure the effects of our minds and the quality of our thoughts. It reveals how positive or harmful words, thoughts and actions impact on our wellbeing and our environment.

In the coming chapters, I will elaborate on how we can make use of the understanding that water can give us, offering an insider's perspective of this magnificent microcosmic world. *The Spirit of Water* will take you deeper into the inner meaning of ice crystal photography as well as some of the practical applications of *hado* in everyday life.

We will explore the following topics:

- An overview of ice crystal photography, including some frequently asked questions regarding how ice crystals form;
- A scientific experiment conducted on ice crystal formation utilizing double-blind conditions;
- The eight classifications of ice crystals, the unique properties of water, its structure and how it bonds, as well as its chemical properties;
- The origins of water and current problems facing the world's water;
- The chemical quality of water as well as different methods of water filtration and purification, and also what constitutes positively-charged water;
- The microcosmic world of water's hexagonal structure and the significance of the hexagon in relation to physical and vibrational purity. This will illustrate some of the primary methods for generating a hexagonal structure in water as well as the health benefits of drinking hexagonally-structured water;
- The hexagonal structure found in nature, as in snowflakes and the hexagonal wax structure of bee hives. We shall look at sacred geometry, numerology and mathematics in relation to the hexagon;
- The origins of healing water and wells around the world where water is reported to have miraculous healing effects;
- How our consciousness, words, images, music and prayer are reflected in water;
- The world of *hado*, the law of sympathetic resonance, and the *hado* of emotions, the senses and how we can relate to our world through the lens of *hado*;
- The *hado* of illness and wellness, and what causes health imbalances;

- The *hado* of cooking and what constitutes positively-charged food;
- A series of practical exercises demonstrating how to use the principles of *hado* in our daily life, including practical meditations and exercises.

Hado is a Japanese word meaning wave motion or vibration. In the context of this book it refers to the subtle energy that exists in the universe.

My personal journey with ice crystals

Many people ask me how I came into contact with Masaru Emoto's work. More than ten years ago I came across a Japanese version of his book *The Messages from Water, Volume 1* on the desk of my local naturopath. It was in Japanese and I couldn't speak the language. But the ice crystal images spoke volumes. I pored over them with the curiosity of a child. After several fruitless attempts to get the book into Australia, I resigned myself to the fact that it was 'not to be'. It would be a few years until the message from water would once again tap me on my shoulder.

The second time I encountered this work was through my Buddhist meditation teacher. During a public lecture he spoke of Emoto's work with a suitable blend of interest and skepticism. I felt that if Emoto's work had caught his attention, there must be something to it.

A few years passed and it was not until the screening of worldwide hit *What the Bleep do we know?!*, which featured his images of ice crystals, that I was tapped a third time. Although the movie presented just a glimpse of these images, it struck me how widely his message had now traveled.

By a strange coincidence, some weeks later a friend of mine rang me to say that he was taking a flight to Los Angles in one week's time to attend Masaru Emoto's *Hado* Instructor School and asked if I would like to come along. Well, I prize myself on being spontaneous, but one week's notice was a little *too* spontaneous. I was nonetheless curious to hear about his trip and eagerly awaited news of his return.

A couple of weeks passed and my friend returned with his eyes wider than ever before. Upon hearing of his experiences I was determined to attend the next instructors' training, wherever it would be. In 2005, Masaru Emoto had begun to offer *Hado* instructor training to Westerners outside Japan and the third *Hado* Instructors' Training was on Big Island, Hawaii. Armed with several questions about the intricate details of the experiments as well as a healthy curiosity, I made the journey to Hawaii. As it turned out I was able to get all my questions answered, despite a series of 'lost in translation' episodes involving a great number of hand gestures and second-hand interpretations through Emoto's translators.

Following my time in training with Masaru Emoto I began to have some interesting experiences in my daily meditations. My mind was all over the place. I experienced a tremendous bout of creativity and began writing down a series of meditations and practices relating to the application of *hado* and ice crystal photography. It was as if something other than myself was writing through me. I had experienced this sort of thing before, but nothing this strong. Over the months that followed, a complete system of practices evolved. I would also receive inspiration in dreams and before going to sleep and waking up. I would keep a notepad and pen beside my bed so I could scribble my inspirations down in the dark, and then I tried to decipher these the following morning.

Following the *Hado* Instructor School in Hawaii (and having been certified as a *Hado* Instructor) I was officially granted permission to share the work of Masaru Emoto. I teamed up with my friend, who had completed the second *Hado* Instructors' School and we decided to form an Australian Institute dedicated to sharing Emoto's work. We decided to call it *Hado* Institute Australia (HIA). What followed was an intensive period of formulating seminar presentations, writing the content for a website and establishing just what we were about.

In April of 2006 I made arrangements to visit IHM in Tokyo with a group of students, so that we could see the offices and laboratory first hand. After navigating our way through the subways of Tokyo, we managed to find Emoto's office. What followed was a tour of the facility and an official welcome from IHM's president Mr Hazaka. Our main aim for visiting IHM was to conduct an experiment on how Reiki affects the tap water of Tokyo. This hadn't been done before. The results and full description of this experiment is detailed in Chapter 6. The results were positive and we had the opportunity to see how IHM functions.

Following my return to Australia, we embarked on a series of seminar presentations in Australia on ice crystal photography and *hado* and we received an encouragingly positive response. We ran workshops on applying the principles of *hado* in daily life and shared the Emoto teachings on water.

In July 2006 Masaru Emoto commenced an Australian tour and I was invited to be his driver during the west coast leg of his tour. After picking him up from the airport we had several hours to pass until his wife arrived early that morning. We discussed *hado* and his vision for a global shift for humanity. It was at this meeting that he suggested that I write the first *hado* book from a western perspective. Embracing his suggestion the result is this book you are now reading.

Since the first ice crystal photograph was taken in September 1994, a small ripple started. This ripple has spread out across the world and has now touched the lives of millions of people. The majority of the ice crystal images presented in this book have been published for the very first time and I would like to thank Masaru Emoto and his team of researchers for entrusting me with the job of sharing this important message.

As you turn the pages I invite you to let the images speak directly to you. Allow some time to reflect. Sink into the vibrational quality of each image. Let the hidden qualities of water speak to you. These natural mandalas are part of you. They represent the potential for peace in our time. I invite you to share them, to make them your own. It is a fascinating and complex topic and I hope you will experience, as I have, the magic of the hidden message of water.

Let me finish this introduction with a traditional Japanese invocation:
moshimo machigaega gozaimashitara arakajime owabi moushi agemasu
"Please forgive me if I've made a mistake."

Lawrence Ellyard
Fremantle, Western Australia, November 2006

PART ONE

CHAPTER 1

ICE CRYSTAL PHOTOGRAPHY

Let us begin with the very foundations that allow us to explore the intricacies of ice crystal photography. We will explore what it is, how ice crystal photographs are taken, the equipment used and the results. For that we need first to look at the innovator and developer of the technique of ice crystal photography, Masaru Emoto. He spent years trying to measure the existence of *hado*, the vibrational pattern that exists in all matter at the sub-atomic level.

In 1994 he had an epiphany, born from reading a single sentence in a scientific book. The sentence read: *"There are no two snowflakes that are alike."* A snow crystal is a solid structure with orderly configured atoms and molecules. Because snow is formed under a variety of conditions, there are no two snow crystals that appear the same. Emoto wondered if this was also the case with crystal structures from the various types of water on the earth. He then came up with a theory that, when water crystallizes, pure water becomes a pure crystal, whereas contaminated water forms disfigured crystals or, in many cases, no crystal is formed.

Emoto thought to himself: "Snow is frozen water. So if we freeze water, water will be crystallized. If we're able to take pictures of water before and after *hado* has been copied into the water (in ice crystal form), the world would become aware of, and accept the existence of, *hado*."

Emoto was confident that his idea would work. After talking about his idea for two months, one of his staff members, a dedicated scientist who had recently joined IHM, responded to Emoto's vision. What followed were several weeks of trial and error with no results. His first attempts to measure *hado* began by utilizing a Radionics device capable of measuring various vibrations of the body at the cellular level. Being successful in reading vibrations through the device was a beginning step but he knew that, in order for people to realize the significance of *hado*, he would need to find a way to measure vibration physically and visually.

No matter what they tried, no ice crystals formed. They tried freezing water through rapid freezing methods, they altered the freezing time and other variables, and more weeks passed. No matter what they did, the frozen water yielded no ice crystal formations. (It was later determined that a freezing time of three hours at -25°C was the optimum freezing time for successful ice crystal results.)

His researcher's confidence in Emoto's idea began to slip, but Emoto knew it would work one day. Fortunately, this researcher enjoyed *sake* (fermented Japanese rice wine) and, at the end of each unsuccessful day, Masaru would take

Figure 1. The first successful micro-cluster ice crystal picture, taken in September 1994

him out for drinks, always optimistic that the results would come. Masaru Emoto often says that his first ice crystal was born from *sake*. One day in September 1994, his researcher came running into his office with his face beaming, holding a picture of the first ice crystal in his hand (see figure 1). "I got it, chief!" he announced. From that day forth they continued taking ice crystal images, with results today numbering in the thousands.

How ice crystal photographs are taken

In order to understand the method of ice crystal photography it is important first to have a basic understanding of *hado*.

Hado is a Japanese word for vibration, and it refers to the fact that everything in the universe has an intrinsic vibratory nature that can be measured. Masaru Emoto discovered that when water was exposed to specific vibrations (*hado*) such as words, music, images and the like, the water reflected this vibratory information in the results when tested.

He found that the stimuli which had a positive vibration yielded a higher volume of structured ice crystals, whereas negative vibrations resulted in distorted, unstructured or a total lack of structured ice crystal formations.

He also tested natural sources of water such as mountain spring water and found that natural sources of water also showed a consistently high number of structured ice crystal formations. However, testing unnatural sources such as tap water from cities yielded negative results.

After thousands of tests under a variety of conditions his research indicated that positive influences on water produce far greater structured ice crystal results than negative influences, whether via natural or human-made influences.

An ice crystal is a solid structure with orderly configured atoms and molecules. Because water is fluid by nature, it is unstable and changes rapidly. In order to obtain an ice crystal, many water samples are required to be photographed. Out of the experiments, Emoto discovered that it was impossible to obtain identical crystal pictures as no two crystals can be perfectly reproduced twice. However, what was discovered were crystals which showed a certain distinctive pattern called a 'grid' or 'laminar' crystal.

These structures enabled a formula for identification based on the crystals' structural tendency. For example, when water was exposed to the words 'I love you' or 'You're cute', hexagonal and harmonious ice crystals formed. When the words 'You make me sick' were exposed to the water samples, distorted, unstructured or a total lack of structured ice crystals formed.

It is important to note that there have been many ice crystal experiments conducted where water that formally had no positive structure was recovered by directing positive outer stimuli. Likewise, positively structured water could be diminished by directing negative outer stimuli. This is explained in greater detail in later chapters.

In order to find an ice crystal, the researcher needs first to obtain a water sample. This water sample can either be a natural source of water, for example a natural spring, or from an unnatural source, for example tap water or distilled water. That is then tested for its purity or pollution, or the researcher uses a water sample and exposes it to outer stimuli such as words, music, images and the like. The water sample is collected in a glass bottle and in the case where an outer stimulus is being tested, the water is exposed to that outer stimulus. An outer stimulus can be playing music to tap water, showing the water a picture or labeling the water container with a word.

Once the water sample has been exposed to the outer stimulus, the water sample is covered so as not to record other information. When the researcher is ready to proceed to the next stage he taps the bottom of the water sample (succussing) to activate the information-content of the water.

Using a syringe, 0.5mls of water are dropped onto fifty Petri dishes, approximately 5cm in diameter (see figure 2). The dishes are then covered and stored in a freezer for three hours at a temperature of -25°C or -13°F (see figure 3). After three hours the Petri Dishes are removed one by one. When they are taken out, ice grains have formed with their center rolled up due to surface tension. They are observed through a dark field electron-microscope in a freezer room at a temperature of -5°C (see figure 4). The grains are very small (less than 0.5cm)

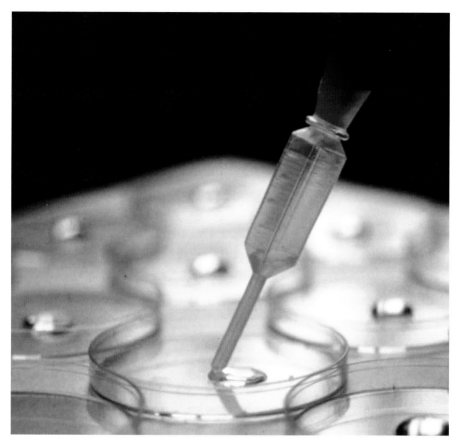

Figure 2. Water droplets dropped into 50 Petri dishes

and it is the very tip of the ice grain which is observed (see figure 5).

Under a magnification of 100 to 200 times, light from the dark-field microscope is directed on a single plane across each grain of ice. If the sample is successful an ice crystal can be observed. Taking only one to two minutes, it opens up like a flower blossoming as the ice begins to melt away.

The fifty Petri dishes contain the same water frozen in the same condition. However, not all ice grains form ice crystals. When we take the photographs, we can categorize the results into groups, such as ice crystals that have many obvious similar hexagonal formations, those that tend to have many collapsed formations and those that have no crystals at all. As we can see from the samples presented in this book, water responds to outer stimuli in forming many different structures acting as a mirror and reflecting and carrying the impressions exposed to it.

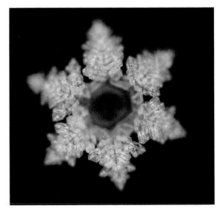

Figure 3. Petri dishes in freezer at -25°C

Figure 4. Olympus System Metal Light Microscope BX60, mounted with an Olympus fully automatic photomicroscope camera PM10SP using Fujicolor professional-quality negative color film, ISO400

Figure 5. Water rolled up when frozen due to surface tension

Figure 6. An example of distilled water shown the word 'chastity'

Eight ice crystal classifications

After more than a decade of research, the researchers at IHM have been able to use a now commonly accepted classification system for ice crystal formations based on commonalities found within the structure of ice crystals. These are classified using the following eight categories.

- Beautiful
- Inclined
- Deformed Hexagon
- Hexagon
- Square
- Indefinite
- Depression
- None

Like snowflakes, no two ice crystals are identical. However, ice crystals do exhibit similar characteristics. Much like family members who share common characteristics such as DNA, physical features and personality traits, so it is similar with ice crystals. After being photographed, the differences and similarities are easily identified.

From fifty Petri dish samples, the researcher may find several different ice crystal formations, depending upon the purity of the water or the success of the influence brought to bear on the water before freezing.

Amongst the ice crystals there may be several examples which come under either of the eight classifications. No class of ice crystals indicates a superior structure to another. Some of the most impressive ice crystals I have seen are 'deformed hexagons' or 'inclined'. Beauty is in the eye of the beholder. Statistically, most people, when judging ice crystal images, find harmonious crystal formations more pleasing, creating positive feelings, compared to less appealing distorted ice crystal images.

When viewing the ice crystal images, notice how each image makes you *feel*.

Some people are quite moved when seeing the ice crystal images for the first time. In some of the *hado* seminars I have conducted, I have observed people experiencing a wide range of emotions from tears to gasps, from laughter to awe.

The following examples are a random selection of ice crystals presented here to illustrate the different classifications. Some of the examples include water which has been exposed to words, to distant intention or to Reiki energy, and some examples are the results of testing tap water. Please enjoy seeing the 'abstract' reflected in these images.

Beautiful

Beautiful ice crystal formations are generally those which form on a horizontal plane, thus making it possible to be photographed as a whole. From above they

Figure 7. A distilled water sample shown the word 'Silence'

have an intact hexagonal structure and symmetrical ferns branching out equally in all directions. The overall symmetry is considered as well as overall harmonious balance and the structure of the ice crystal.

Figure 7 is an example of a Beautiful ice crystal. Here the water was exposed to the vibration of the word 'Silence', in the sense of quiet and stillness, not the command 'SILENCE!'. When water is shown a command such as 'DO IT!', only distorted formations appear, where as the statement 'Let's do it' or 'Let's do it together' creates beautiful ice crystal formations.

Inclined

An inclined ice crystal is almost perfect in symmetry and balance, yet it exhibits some imperfections in its appearance. An example is shown in figure 8 where water was shown the words 'thank you' in Hebrew. Although this ice crystal shows a lack of perfect symmetry as well as a slight imbalance in the hexagonal structure it is nevertheless an impressive looking example.

Figure 8. A distilled water sample shown the words 'thank you' in Hebrew

Hexagon

Hexagon ice crystals are crystals where the predominate feature is a hexagon (as the name suggests). Hexagonal ice crystals exhibit a clean simplicity and evoke a Zen-like quality. Figure 9 is an ice crystal of water shown the words 'thank you' in Serbo-Croat. No matter what the language, the *hado* or vibrational quality of 'thank you' is universal.

Figure 9. A distilled water sample shown the words 'thank you' in Serbo-Croat

Deformed Hexagon

A deformed hexagon indicates an ice crystal with multiple hexagons or a significant break in the hexagonal structure. Some of the most striking examples of deformed hexagon ice crystals reveal a beauty of their own, such as tap water shown the words 'love and thanks', as in figure 10.

Figure 10. A tap water sample shown the words 'love and thanks'

Square

A square ice crystal shows a formation without a hexagonal structure. Square structure ice crystals offer an alternative view of ice crystals and have a unique characteristic of their own. An example of a square ice crystal is illustrated in figure 11 from Tokyo tap water. Tokyo tap water never forms structured ice crystals due to the vibratory quality of the water as well as the high level of chlorine within the water.

Figure 11. An example of a square ice crystal taken from tap water in Tokyo, Japan

Indefinite

This category indicates some rather unusual examples of ice crystal formations. They are neither hexagonal nor square. Ice crystal formations exhibiting these qualities are in a unique class of their own and do not fit into any of the other classifications. Figure 12 is an example of an Indefinite ice crystal formation.

Depression

Although an unfortunate label, 'depression' relates to a compressed or suffocating-looking ice crystal formation. Ice crystals exhibiting these results are often associated with formations where the water sample lacks purity or has been exposed to negative vibrations, such as angry words or electromagnetic frequencies from such things as mobile phones, computer monitors or microwave ovens (see chapter 7). When observing these formations, they actually look depressed.

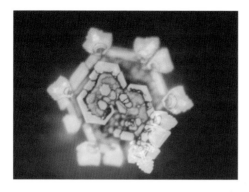

Figure 12. An 'indefinite' ice crystal formation. Water exposed to Reiki energy as part of a group healing experiment. See Chapter 6 for more on this experiment

They are highly irregular and reflect a lack of structure or hexagonal form. Figure 13 is an example of an 'Depression' ice crystal formation.

None

As this name suggests, no discernable ice crystal can be found. It is common to chlorinated tap water or water exposed to negative stimuli such as negative words. Figure 14 shows a sample of tap water from the city of Bangkok. Once again we see a total lack of structure. The

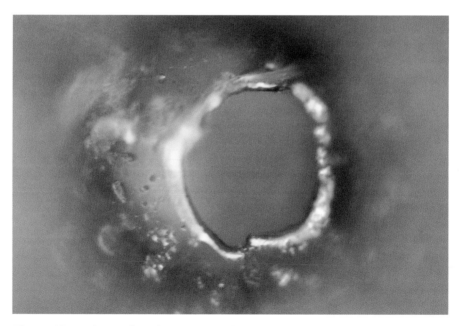

Figure 13. A 'depression' formation. This is a crystal from the city of Sydney's tap water, observed under a microscope

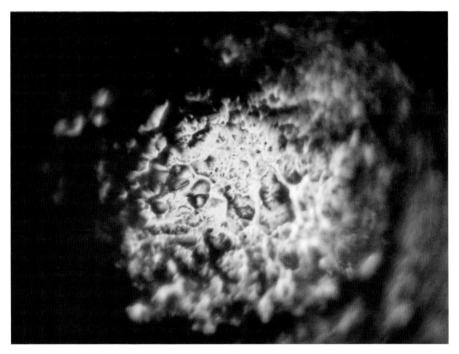

Figure 14. The results of tap water from the city of Bangkok, Thailand, observed under the microscope.

result illustrates the chemical quality of Bangkok's water as well as its vibrational quality.

As we can see from the eight classifications, there is a great variety of possible forms and structures. It is not until we look at several hundred samples that we start to see what is referred to as 'family' crystals. Family crystals are those where samples exhibit a similar structure and appearance to each other, such as the ice crystals for 'love and gratitude' (figure 61) and 'cleanliness' (figure 41). These ice crystals look familiar in their characteristics, and hence they are classified into crystal families.

CHAPTER 2

FREQUENTLY ASKED QUESTIONS ABOUT ICE CRYSTALS

Since the first book on Masaru Emoto's work, *The Message from Water*, was published in June 1999, there have been many questions asked about ice crystal photographic methodology and how *hado* is measured and transferred into water. There has also been understandable doubt from the mainstream scientific community.

Toward the end of this chapter I have addressed some of the issues surrounding ice crystal photography as well as details of the first scientific double-blind experiment conducted by Masaru Emoto and Dean Radin of the Noetic Sciences Institute (USA), in 2006. It was a significant accomplishment, since a double-blind trial is considered one of the best methods for obtaining objective scientific validation and it is accepted as the gold standard by many scientists and researchers.

The following most frequently asked questions have been collected from a variety of people from scientific and other backgrounds.

Out of fifty Petri dish samples, do all 50 produce an ice crystal?
To answer this question we need to look at the different samples utilized in the experiment. What can be said is that the greater the purity of the sample or the more positive the stimuli leaving an impression on the water, the greater the success rate in producing a variety of ice crystal formations.

When water is exposed to stimuli it absorbs and holds this information. This information or vibration can be called *hado*, which can be measured as negative, positive or neutral in vibration. When water is exposed to any type of vibration it responds by forming either a greater or lesser amount of structured ice crystal formations. Exposed to negative stimuli, the water has a tendency to produce less harmonious or beautiful-type ice crystals. When exposed to positive stimuli, the water has a tendency to produce a greater amount of beautiful-type ice crystals.

To illustrate this point, let us examine an experiment conducted near a small village in Thailand. Water was collected in the rainy season and placed in three jars in three distinct locations. The object of the experiment was to determine whether there would be variation in the quality and number of ice crystal formations, depending upon where the water was stored. The hypothesis was, "Is water influenced by the *hado* of different environments?"

The first location was in the grounds of a village. The second was in the rainforest just outside the village and the third in the Buddhist temple grounds near the village (where meditation was practiced).

What was found was the number of ice crystals formations varied greatly. The village sample produced five beautiful-type ice crystals out of fifty samples with a 10% success rate – see figure 15. The rainforest sample produced nine beautiful-type ice crystals out of fifty samples with an 18% success rate – see figure 16. The temple sample produced twelve beautiful-type ice crystals out of 50 samples, with a 24% success rate – see figure 17.

What does this show us? The lower number of ice crystal formations in the village sample suggests that the day-to-day experiences of the villagers include

Figure 15. Rainwater kept in the grounds of a village in Thailand

Figure 16. Rainwater kept in the forest near a village in Thailand

Figure 17. Rainwater kept in the temple grounds near a village in Thailand

positive as well as negative impressions, which in turn affected the vibratory quality of the water. Thus, the result was a lower number of ice crystal formations than in the other samples. The *hado* was not very clear or strong in this environment.

The rainforest water, being kept in a more pure environment and unaffected by human disturbing influences, produced a higher number of ice crystals. The positive and unpolluted *hado* of the natural environment imbued the water with a higher vibration. Thus, the result was a greater number of ice crystal formations.

The water stored in the temple grounds produced the highest number of beautiful-type ice crystal formations. The reason was the positively-charged environment where the water jars were kept. The daily chanting of the monks and their calm and humble disposition had a direct effect on the water sample, thus rendering the highest ice crystal result.

This experiment reflects back to us the importance of the vibratory quality of any environment. A natural, healthy environment results in beautiful ice crystals, but a positive human influence can alter and increase the already positive *hado* of a place, producing the greatest results and the highest amounts of structured ice crystals.

Are ice crystals static or do they grow?

The images in this book show a still image of ice crystals but, when observed under the microscope, they are in fact still growing. This is due to a rise in temperature while the crystals are being photographed. As soon as one of the ice droplets of the 50 samples is removed from the freezer at -25°C and placed under the microscope in the freezer room at -5°C, the rise in temperature causes the ice droplet to expand. Ice crystals form at the very tip of the ice droplet so this is the place which is observed. As the temperature continues to rise, the ice slowly begins to melt. The researcher observes the entire process, which takes from two to three minutes. If a sample is positive, containing an ice crystal, it will appear at the very tip of the ice droplet in a tiny point. Magnified over 200 times this point will begin to blossom, much like a flower. Influenced by the temperature rise and using high speed photography, the unfoldment of ice crystals is captured on film. Figure 18 shows a lateral view of an ice droplet, with an ice crystal formation growing at the tip.

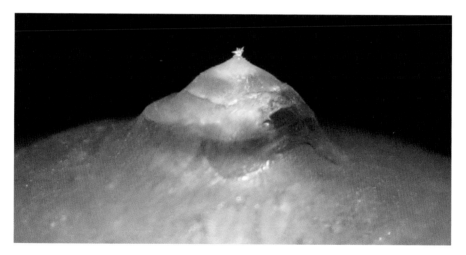

Figure 18. Lateral view of an ice droplet, with an ice crystal formation growing at the tip

From the tip of the ice droplet (which can exhibit a hexagonal core), ferns may begin to radiate outwards. In the space of just a few minutes we observe the birth, life and death of an ice crystal. The researcher captures a sequence of images of one unfolding ice crystal using the camera mounted on the microscope. Eventually the ice droplet melts completely and is lost forever.

Using time-lapse film, the ice crystal's movement can be observed from beginning to end.

Do ice crystals always grow horizontally?

You may have noticed when observing the ice crystal images in this book that some show a section in focus whilst other parts are more blurred. The reason is that all ice crystals grow three-dimensionally. Imagine a Christmas tree with a star on the top, and imagine that the tree is photographed from an aerial perspective right above the center. If only the top of the photo is in focus, the bottom ferns would appear blurry on film, due to camera's 'depth of field'. As a camera can only photograph one plane under the microscope, the entire ice crystal is in many cases not in focus.

The best person to observe the growth of an ice crystal is the researcher. The birth, life and death of an ice crystal unfolds before the researcher's eyes and takes place within two to three minutes – a short life by anyone's standard.

In some cases ice crystals grow at an angle unseen with the microscope. In other samples they may only be partially viewable. When ice crystals grow at an angle, only a section or the top side of an otherwise perfect ice crystal formation can be observed by the researcher. Thus the limitations of viewing a three-dimensional form on a two-dimensional plane leads to photographic shortcomings.

Can the researcher influence the water samples?

Although the researcher tries to remain balanced and objective, it is possible to influence water samples when handling them, especially when the researcher is dropping water droplets into the Petri dishes.

One of the IHM researchers told me of an instance where his state of mind influenced the results. One day he happened to be in a bad mood. When he was dropping the water into the Petri dishes and photographing the results, almost all of the ice crystals grew away from him.

Therefore it is important that the researcher does his best to remain objective and does not add further stimuli to the existing water sample. This can be readily achieved at IHM as all of the Japanese researchers speak little or no English. When water samples are brought in for testing the water samples are mostly labeled in another language, thus reducing subjective influence by the researcher. However this is not to say that all water samples are not known by the researchers but, in most cases, they aim to maintain a neutral state of mind when conducting the experiments.

Some other factors include the person labeling the bottle, the expectations of the researchers or of others involved with the results of the experiment. Distance also has a potential bearing on the outcome: consciousness is not bound by time or space, so if we focus our intention on water sitting right in front of us or on the other side of the earth, the result or effect remains roughly the same.

This has been quantified several times through IHM experiments in which water was influenced at great distances. To make the assumption that every ice crystal experiment is performed under strict double-blind conditions is therefore incorrect. There are times when both the person performing the experiment and the person who is responsible for sending in the water sample can influence the results. However, statistically it has been observed that water forms more ice crystals when it receives positive stimuli and less when negative stimuli are directed to it.

Many scientific researchers have scoffed at the research into consciousness absorbed by water, and have simply discounted it as pseudo-science without looking into the full body of this work. As more experiments and more double-blind studies under controlled conditions are conducted, there surely will be a wider acceptance to Emoto's work.

When water has been exposed to outer influences, how long does that influence stay in the water?

Water has the ability to hold information, both positive and negative. If water is exposed to negative stimuli the result will generally stay as long as the surrounding environment continues to support a negative energy field. If we have water which is exposed to positive stimuli, yet it is kept in a negative environment, then the positive effects will decrease sooner than they would in an otherwise neutral environment. If the positive influence is continually maintained both in the environment and inwardly through continued conscious intention, then the positive influence will not only remain, but it will continue to increase, resulting in a higher percentage of ice crystal formations in any given 50 samples.

Water also has an ability to recover. If structured water is exposed to negative influences, it loses its structure. But direct a positive influence into it and the water once again recovers its structure.

Criticism of ice crystal photography from the scientific community

As with any new science there are many who question the validity of Emoto's work. Masaru Emoto does not make any claims that his research is based upon a mainstream scientific approach, yet his results are very convincing and make sense to a lot of people. In this section we will look at the common statements of opposition to his discovery and present some answers and explanations to these challenges.

It is often the case that, when research involves consciousness and the 'quantum' world, there may be more shades of grey than clear, black-and-white answers. Therefore answers can arise which are considered 'both/and', as opposed to 'either/or' in nature. However at the same time they can be more satisfying and be an eye-opener to a greater science yet to be fully understood.

The following are some of the more frequently asked questions concerning Emoto's research.

Challenge 1: *Water holding memory*

Claims do not come much more controversial than the idea that water might retain a memory of substances. This very notion is central to the practice of Homeopathy, which treats patients vibrationally. The medicinal substance is dissolved in water and is then diluted many times, to the extent that it is unlikely to contain a single molecule of the active compound. Yet there is still an effect when the remedy is taken. This is because the water contains a memory of the substance – and, according to homeopathic principles, the memory or vibration is more potent in effect than the substance.

Homeopathy is based on the principle of 'like treats like'. In other words, to treat an ailment, a homeopathically-potentized amount of a poison or a potentially harmful element is often given, which stimulates a body-mind reaction both to the 'medicine' and to the ailment, thus curing the ailment. The remedy jogs the body-mind system into action.

The 'memory of water' phenomenon has largely been ignored by mainstream science, and there has been little scientific enquiry and conventional research undertaken to understand it. There are a few exceptions. Present day researchers such as David Schweitzer, Prof Jacques Benveniste, Dr Wolfgang Ludwig and Viktor Schauberger have all contributed research quantifying water's marvelous properties. It is said that water is the most programmable substance in the world. Unlike any other substance water has an ability to retain an energetic signature of whatever is placed in it.

The work of Masaru Emoto takes this notion in a new direction through ice crystal photography. Through observing visual form in ice crystals, his research reveals microscopically that water does indeed have an ability to hold memory. Water is like a blank CD which can record, store and even transmit information. It can store and transfer information within the human body, which is made largely of water. Emoto's research highlights the ability of water to store vibrations, whether this water comes from a mountain stream or from a poorer source which has then been exposed to a positive influence such as that of a flower.

Water molecules have both a positive and negative pole and they behave in a similar way to magnets. Water molecules are attracted to other water molecules which then form clusters numbering in the hundreds. The clustered molecules are receptive to information and thus store data or memory which can be transmitted to other water sources. For example, water with a pure *hado* can be added to the water source of a city's water supply or to a polluted lake, thereby assisting in recovery of the quality of the larger body of water. The recovery of lakes and rivers through the use of *hado* is now conducted through a variety of projects under the guidance of Masaru Emoto.

Water also has qualities which go beyond simple chemistry. It has an ability to hold information and this effect is known as *epitaxy*. Epitaxy is where the atomic structure of one compound is used as a template to induce the same structure in others.

Most mainstream scientists dismiss homeopathy as simply a placebo effect. The reason why homeopathy is not a placebo is due to water's ability to form these sensitive molecular structures which are impressionable to outer vibrational influences. Every substance and element has its own vibrational pattern, which is today widely accepted through ongoing research in quantum physics. This vibrational pattern is imprinted into water in homeopathic remedies and taken by the patient. This same vibrational pattern interacts with the imbalance in the patient through a transfer process via the molecular cluster holding the vibrational pattern – in this case, in the homeopathic medicine. The vibrational pattern stored in water merges with the water in our body, even without a trace of the original physical substance being present. By taking the remedy regularly until symptoms disappear we keep reminding the water in our body what vibration it should have, until finally it has changed back to its healthy state.

Challenge 2: *Ice crystals cannot be replicated*

No two ice crystals are exactly the same. For any phenomenon to be scientifically validated it needs to be reproducible. However, in order for mainstream science to validate the ice crystal phenomenon a paradigm shift in the notion of reproducibility must be made. The reproducibility model simply does not fit the nature of ice crystal formation.

Singularity, or the observation that no two things are the same, is a common characteristic of nature. To remove the singularity principle in nature makes any mainstream scientific testing of natural phenomena under natural circumstances very difficult. Emoto's discoveries are based on the principle of singularity and as such do not fit the scientific parameters of reproducibility.

With the birth of the industrial age some 200 years ago, there was a shift in the mainstream scientific community from a blend of scientific enquiry embodying a more all-round understanding of nature, both metaphysical and material, toward a purely rational materialistic understanding of the universe. To discount the ice crystal phenomena as 'new-age nonsense' because of the ice crystals' singularity is unreasonable.

Challenge 3: *Ice crystal samples are hand-selected and therefore subjective*

When one water sample is divided into fifty small droplet samples, there will often be several droplets that differ substantially from most ice crystals in the sample. Out of these, Masaru Emoto personally selects ice crystal images which he feels represent the stimuli that the water was exposed to. This does indeed make this part of the selection process subjective. There are of course many ways to interpret an ice crystal, and each ice crystal will elicit a varying response from the person viewing the ice crystal images. It is thus useful for that person to view the images without knowing what influences have been applied to them, so that images are selected purely on the basis of a judgment of quality, not of their significance. Afterwards, when the selection has been made, a knowledge of the influences applied will help in interpreting the value of the experiment.

Challenge 4: *Samples are digitally enhanced and created electronically*

Although digital imaging would save a great deal of time and expense, the researches at IHM use only Fujicolor professional-quality negative color film (ISO 400). On top of each microscope is mounted an Olympus fully automatic photomicroscope camera (PH10 SP).

Using film as opposed to digital images ensures originality and a capacity to verify that the images shot on film are authentic. Some years ago, a group of scientists tried to debunk Masaru Emoto's research on the basis that it was nothing more than clever digitally-manipulated imaging. They suggested that all of the ice crystal images were created in Photoshop using computer effects. This matter was taken to court and Emoto's case was won when all of the original films were presented. This proved beyond a shadow of a doubt that no digital imaging had been used.

Double-blind experiment
demonstrating distant intention on ice crystal formation

Since Masaru Emoto first began to publish his research in 1994, he attracted a great deal of support as well as a healthy amount of criticism surrounding the validity of ice crystal photography and the ability of water to reflect intention. The need for a scientifically objective double-blind test has been sought for many years. This level of scientific testing has now been conducted with positive results, confirming what millions of people around the world have always believed but could not scientifically quantify.

On November 16th 2005, in a collaboration between Masaru Emoto and Dean Radin of the Noetic Sciences Institute in California, a double-blind test was conducted on the effects of distant intention on water crystal formation. The results of this experiment were first published in *Explore* Journal in September 2006 (Vol 2, 5). *Explore* is an interdisciplinary journal that investigates the healing arts, consciousness, spirituality, eco-environmental issues and basic science.

The hypothesis: to see what effect sending positive intention over a large distance could have on water.

In preparation, four plastic bottles of Fiji brand commercial bottled water were used. Bottles labeled A and B were used in the experiment and bottles labeled C and D were used in the control groups. This brand of water was selected because, unlike many other bottled waters, after the Fiji label was removed, the plastic bottle contained no words, symbols or other shapes embossed in the plastic.

A group of approximately 2,000 people in Tokyo simultaneously projected positive intention towards water samples located inside an electromagnetically-sealed room in California. That same group was unaware of the existence of similar water samples (bottles C and D) set aside in a different location at the Noetic Sciences Institute as the control samples. Neither did the researchers doing the analysis know which sample was being treated by intention, thus ensuring the double-blind part of the study.

Masaru Emoto led the group in Tokyo in a prayer of gratitude directed to the water in the IONS laboratory, some 5,000 miles away, for approximately five minutes. In order for the group participating in the experiment to have something to focus their intention upon, a digital photo of the water samples (bottles A and B) was e-mailed to Masaru Emoto to be used as a visual aid.

Figures 19 and 20. Results from the distant intention experiment on ice crystal formation from water sample groups A and B

Figures 21 and 22. Results from distant intention experiment on ice crystal formation from control water sample groups C and D

The four water samples were then sent to the IHM research laboratory to be tested. When photographed, both groups of water had formed ice crystals, but the group which had received the positive intention produced far greater results. The ice crystal images were then shown to a group of 100 independent judges, who rated how aesthetically pleasing all of the crystals appeared. They did not know which water samples the images came from.

The study showed that the water that had positive intention sent to it over a large distance displayed crystals that were judged to be more aesthetically pleasing than the water that did not have positive intentions sent to it. The difference between the two samples was significant.

The two images in figures 19 and 20 were random samples from the water which had been sent positive intention (bottles A and B). The images in figures 21 and 22 were photos taken of the water from the control group (bottles C and D).

The results of this scientific study clearly illustrate that our intention can affect and change water. Being the first double-blind study of this kind, the results are by no means accepted to be conclusive, but with further studies in the future perhaps more of the scientific community will acknowledge ice crystal research of this kind.

For a full description of this experiment, see the appendix section at the end of this book.

CHAPTER 3

ALL ABOUT WATER

Before we turn to the implications of Masaru Emoto's discoveries and how they apply to us today, let us first gain further understanding of water. It is perhaps the single most important substance on the planet, for the simple reason that, without it, there would be no life. This precious substance has numerous uses apart from drinking. It is used for washing, cooling, heating, the disposal of wastes and for several industrial, medicinal and scientific purposes.

The way we relate to water today is a far cry from the relationship our ancestors had with it. Water was respected and revered, worshiped as the bringer of life, the feminine principle, giving life to all. But today water is seen largely as a commodity. Bottled water is a multi-billion dollar industry and in some countries it is even becoming more expensive than oil. There seems to be a great desire and need to consume natural or unpolluted water and it seems people are willing to pay for it.

One of the major problems we are facing in the world today is the lack of pure water. Since the industrial age, we have increasingly accelerated levels of pollution and our pure water sources are being lost. Of course water is everywhere, but much of it is unusable for consumption.

The work of Masaru Emoto brings with it a powerful message. It is a wake-up call for all of us. Through his images of ice crystals, we are being shown that what we do, say and think really matters. In our busy world it is all too easy to get caught up in day-to-day survival, making money, working a job, having relationships, buying and selling, raising families, and we have forgotten how to slow down, pause a moment and think what life is really about.

The spirit of water speaks to all of us. It does not adjust what it reveals to shelter us from the reality we face but shows us an uncompromising glimpse of reality. Good and bad, pure and impure, this message brings with it a choice. We have a need to choose how we view reality and we have infinite possibilities to co-create a world worth living in. This begins with each one of us.

The origins of water

Over the years there have been many scientific theories regarding the origins of water but perhaps the most intriguing, aided by a recent discovery, is that the Earth's water may have come from outer space. In 1997 a press report from NASA announced: "We observed for the first time a snowball-shaped microscopic heavenly body flying in numerous numbers towards the stratosphere of Earth from space... About a few thousand of them come flying in daily but, as they come near the Earth's surface, they decompose and become part of the clouds."

In other words, the findings suggest that rain is falling daily from space. Although this vapor may be very small in volume, over a period of 4.6 billion years it may have been enough to create the Earth's oceans and thus it could also have seeded the origins of life on Earth. Additional research was announced by the astronomical observatory on Big Island, Hawaii, offering similar findings. The crucial observations were made on November 26, 2005, using the 8-meter Gemini North telescope on Mauna Kea, Big Island, Hawaii.

The Earth is believed to have formed hot and dry, meaning that its current water content must have been delivered after the planet cooled. Possible candidates for supplying this water are colliding comets and asteroids. Because of their large ice content, comets were leading candidates for many years, but recent analysis of comet water has shown that comet water is significantly different from typical ocean water on Earth.

If the origin of Earth's water is space, as is being suggested, and if that same water comprises roughly 70% of our bodies, is it not plausible to suggest that we might also be of this origin? The more we research water, the more that clues may arise to suggest its origin.

The properties of water

Unlike any other substance, the properties of water are unique. We are all familiar with water's chemical description, H_2O. But what does this actually mean? One atom of oxygen is bound to two atoms of hydrogen. The hydrogen atoms are attached to one side of the oxygen atom, meaning that a water molecule has a positive charge on the side where the hydrogen atoms are located and a negative charge on the side where the oxygen atom is. Since opposite electrical charges attract, water molecules tend to attract each other, making water, for want of a better term, 'sticky'.

When observing a water droplet it raises like a dome or half-sphere (figure 23), thanks to surface tension. In zero gravity this half-sphere would in fact be a perfect sphere. What we observe as a half-sphere is only the earth's gravity holding it down.

Figure 23. An example of the surface tension of water forming beads on a leaf

Since the hydrogen and oxygen atoms in a molecule carry opposite charges, nearby water molecules are attracted to each other like tiny magnets. The electrostatic attraction between the hydrogen and the oxygen in adjacent molecules is called 'hydrogen bonding'.

Hydrogen bonding makes water molecules 'stick' together. While hydrogen bonds are relatively weak compared to other types of bonds, they are strong enough to give water many unique properties. When several of these water molecules are attracted together they form clumps or drops. In water's liquid form, hydrogen bonding pulls water molecules together. As a result, liquid water has a relatively compact, dense structure. On the flip side, as water freezes into ice, the molecules become frozen in place and begin to arrange themselves in a rigid lattice structure.

Here are some further aspects of water's properties:

- Water is unique in that it is the only natural substance that is found in all three states, under natural conditions – in the form of liquid (water), solid (ice) and gas (steam or vapor).
- Water is constantly in motion and interacting through evaporation into vapor, condensation into liquid and back again, always in a constant cycle.
- Water freezes at $0°C$ or $32°F$ and boils at $100°C$ or $212°F$. Water's freezing and boiling points are the baseline with which temperature is measured.
- Water is unusual in that the solid form, ice, is less dense than the liquid form, which is why ice floats. If ice didn't have this quality, the ice in your glass would sink to the bottom or, worse, the fish in your pond would have a very bad day.
- Water has a high specific heat index. This means that water can absorb a lot of heat before it begins to get hot. This is why water is valuable to industries for cooling and in your car's radiator as a coolant. Equally, in central heating systems it loses heat gradually. The high specific heat index of water also helps regulate the rate at which air temperature changes, which is why temperature change in moister climates between seasons and between day and night is gradual rather than sudden, especially near the oceans.
- Water has a very high surface tension. It is sticky and elastic, tending to clump together in drops rather than spread out in a thin film. Molecules at the surface of liquid water have fewer neighbors and, as a result, have a greater

attraction to any water molecules that are nearby. This enhanced attraction is called surface tension. It makes the surface of the liquid slightly more difficult to break through than the interior. When a light object that would normally sink in water is placed carefully on the surface, it can remain suspended on the surface due to surface tension. Surface tension is responsible for capillary action, which allows water and its dissolved substances to move through the roots of plants and through the tiny blood vessels in our bodies.

- Water is a universal solvent. It can dissolve more substances than any other liquid. Water is the ideal transporter of minerals, whether through the ground or through our bodies, and it carries anything soluble, be it matter, vibration, information and even electromagnetic waves.

How much water is there?

The Earth is very much a 'closed system', meaning that the Earth neither gains nor loses much matter, including its water. Some matter, such as meteors from outer space, are captured by the Earth, yet very little of Earth's substances escape into outer space. This is certainly true about water. This means that the same water that existed on Earth millions of years ago is still here today and is continually being recycled around the globe. So it is entirely possible that the water you drank today was once flowing in the Amazon river thousands of years ago.

It is estimated that there is approximately 1.3 to 1.4 billion cubic kilometers or 326 million cubic miles of water on the planet. A cubic mile of water equals more than one trillion gallons.

Of this, 97.5% is salt water, 2.09% is frozen and 0.4% is fresh water. Of the fresh water only 0.01% is directly available for drinking water, and much of this is not considered clean or pure water.

About 3,100 cubic miles of water, mostly in the form of water vapor, is in the atmosphere at any one time. If it all fell as precipitation at once, the Earth would be covered with only about 1 inch or 2.5cm of water.

The problems facing water

One of the biggest problems facing water is contamination of drinking water in developing countries. It is estimated that 1.2 billion people on the planet today do not have access to clean and safe drinking water. More than 2.5 billion people have no access to treating water to improve its quality.

United Nations reports indicate that over 4,000 children die each day from a lack of clean water whereas, in the United States, if we were to take an average of the population of North America, each person uses approximately 522 liters of clean drinking water per day. If we were to include industry this increases to 805 liters per person per day (based on a 2003 National Report).

The United States is also the leader in power and resources consumption and, as a consequence, the biggest contributor to greenhouse emissions. Ironically, the United States is one of two countries yet to ratify the Kyoto protocol on climate change, the other being Australia.

In Australia, a country where water is considered scarce, Australians use an average of 256 liters per day and, with the inclusion of industry, a total of 440 liters per person per day. Over 70% is used by agriculture. The remaining 30% is shared by households, manufacturing, mining, electricity, gas and the national water service. Only 8% is used by householders and, of that, the greatest amount is used in the bathroom.

For years, a 'use water wisely' advertising campaign has been running and is something which today is ingrained into the minds of every Australian. We do have a national responsibility to make sure we do not waste water. This is a wonderful ethos which has been embraced nationally. The more we can begin to foster a relationship to water as something sacred, the more this responsibility will be engendered and, collectively, with increased awareness, we can not only improve the quality of water but also improve the fair consumption of this precious resource.

The state of the world's water

It has been estimated that on Earth today there are around 120,000 types of chemicals with around 1,000 new chemical combinations being created each year. A staggering 800 different chemicals have been found in drinking water in various parts of the world.

Through a variety of means these chemicals find their way into our rivers, lakes and streams, adding to an already polluted environment. Because water is absorbent, it can absorb soluble chemicals which are mostly unseen by the naked eye. To illustrate just how soluble water is you can conduct a simple experiment called the Salt and Pepper Test (see figure 24). Take two glasses of tap water. Into one glass add a half teaspoon of table salt and stir for one minute. Now observe the glass. In most cases all of the salt which was originally in solid form has been absorbed into the water. Although you cannot see it, you can definitely taste it. Now take a half teaspoon of ground pepper. Stir this for one minute. You will observe that the particles do not dissolve and are either suspended within the water or floating on the surface (due to surface tension). This experiment demonstrates the difference between soluble and non-soluble substances.

In the same way, just because you cannot see most chemicals which are in your tap water, it does not mean they are not present. If you are drinking tap water on a regular basis you are inevitability absorbing chemicals into your body

Figure 24. The salt and pepper test

and bloodstream. Although the body has some built in methods to purify and expel chemical contaminants, there are some it cannot filter. Let us now look at some of the potential chemicals found in tap water.

Some of the contaminates found in water include chlorine, trihalomethanes, chemicals such as weedkiller or pesticides, polyaromatic hydrocarbons (PAHs), lead, aluminum, cadmium and fluoride. The following is a more detailed description.

Chlorine

Chlorine is by far one of the best ways to eradicate bacteria. As a result, in the developed world we no longer have to deal with outbreaks of cholera and typhoid, but chlorine brings with it a whole range of problems. *The American Journal of Public Health* estimates that approximately 9% of bladder cancers and 15% of rectal cancers are linked by the longterm consumption of drinking chlorine-treated tap water.

The term 'chlorinated' water is in fact a little misleading. When chlorine is mixed with water, hypochlorous acid forms. It is the hypochlorous acid that kills bacteria, not the chlorine itself. You may be concerned to know that the active ingredient in household bleach is a form of hypochlorous acid, which by nature is very reactive. Because of its reactivity, the chlorine kills bacteria but can also create other potentially hazardous chemicals, especially when mixed with organic chemicals existing in most water sources. This can create several cancer-causing agents such as chloroform, bromoform and bromodichloromethane.

Although chlorination removes bacteria, it has an adverse effect on the water molecules at the molecular level. Chlorination causes unnaturally large clusters, which causes the structure of the water to become unbalanced. When water becomes unbalanced it reduces water's capacity to carry nutrients to the cells in our body and to remove toxins and waste from the body. The water also becomes less oxygenated.

One of the most noticeable and striking results from chlorinated water samples seen under the microscope is their visible lack of hexagonal structure.

In all but a few cases, most tap water in the major cities around the world fails to generate a strong hexagonal structure as observed in ice crystals. Except for a few cities surrounded by mountains or glaciers and drawing a high percentage of their water form these sources, chlorinated water is one of the major obstacles to forming structured water.

When it comes to bathing in water, without a shower filter you might be surprised to know that heat assists heavy metals to dissolve in water. To give an example, just ten minutes in the shower or thirty minutes in a bath of chlorinated tap water can contribute to a greater intake of chemical cocktails than drinking 4 liters of chlorinated tap water.

Chlorinated tap water is absorbed through the body's largest organ, the skin. It is also absorbed through inhalation. Although the human body has a built-in filter, the liver, it can only filter the blood. When we are submerged in chlorinated water, many of these chemicals enter the body and other vital organs long before reaching the liver, and therefore they can be considerably bad for one's health. An alternative to 'chemical bath-time' is to install a carbon filter into your shower or home water supply. Carbon filters can remove a great many contaminants from tap water, and your skin and hair will feel and smell much nicer.

Trihalomethanes

Trihalomethanes are poisonous compounds formed when chlorine reacts with dissolved chemicals, especially pesticides. Chloroform, for example is a trihalomethane. They are carcinogenic and can damage cell structures in living organisms, not least human beings.

Agricultural chemicals

Agricultural chemicals are increasingly finding their way into our water systems and oceans. Although there are standards set in countries like USA and in Europe, new chemicals are being developed and put into use long before their longterm effects can be fully quantified.

Polyaromatic Hydrocarbons (PAHs)

Polyaromatic hydrocarbons (PAHs) are derived from asphalt, which is used as a coating inside cast-iron pipes to prevent corrosion. Unfortunately, PAHs are highly carcinogenic. Some PAHs can dissolve into tap water. PAHs can also enter groundwater from ash, tar or creosote that has been is improperly disposed of in landfills.

Lead

For the most part high lead content in water is not so much an issue at the source, but is a problem picked up along the way through old pipes made from lead, or from the lead solder used for joining pipes. Excessive lead in water can lead to learning difficulties in children, as well as problems associated with fetal development in pregnant women. Other problems associated with excessive lead include hypertension, strokes and heart disease. As lead is stored in the body, it takes years to eliminate it. Lead is toxic to many of our body's tissues and enzymes. Children particularly are susceptible to lead poisoning because it can accumulate in their nervous system as their bodies grow and develop.

Aluminum

Aluminum is strongly linked with Alzheimer's Disease. Think again if you are using aluminum drinking flasks or cooking with aluminum pots and pans. Aluminum is included in the 2005 list of top priority toxins in the United States (a list put out every year by the Agency for Toxic Substances & Disease Registry). Aluminum has been clearly identified as a toxin for the human nervous system (neuro-toxicity), immune system (immuno-toxicity), and genetic system (geno-toxicity).

Cadmium

Cadmium can be found in water where houses have zinc-plated pipes. Much like lead, it is stored in the body and can lead to kidney failure, liver damage and severe stomach cramps.

Fluoride

In Western Europe most countries have rejected water fluoridation, including Austria, Belgium, Denmark, Finland, France, Germany, Italy, Luxembourg, Netherlands, Norway and Sweden. The predominant reason for Europe's rejection of fluoride is the view that public drinking water is not an appropriate vehicle with which to deliver medication to the general population. Countries like India and Japan have also either rejected or banned its use in recent years.

Respected medical professionals and scientists warn that water fluoridation has dangerous longterm consequences to one's health. However, for over fifty years the US government and popular media have heralded fluoride as a safe and effective means of reducing cavities, especially in children. But fluoride is not the benevolent and innocuous substance the public has long been led to believe.

Children who take fluoride daily can actually suffer tooth and bone decalcification and, as a result, this can lead to 'Fluorosis'. Fluoride is very reactive substance and penetrates deep into the bones and cells, where it accumulates. Further research indicates that fluoride causes joint problems, skeletal deformations, osteoporosis and may even lead to bone cancer. Fluoride has a negative influence on the nervous system and immune system. In children it can lead to chronic fatigue, a reduced IQ, learning disabilities, lethargy and depression.

When we expose ourselves to water with so many impurities we make our body vulnerable to the potential side-effects of drinking impure water. By attending to correct methods of filtration as well as positively charging water with consciousness, we will reap the rewards for both our body and mind.

Drinking water standards

We know water can vary according to location and the substances found within it, but many are not aware of the ways water is generically classified. With so much variation in the standard of drinking water it is important to know how water is rated. The quality of drinking water is generally classified under the following five categories:

1. the physical quality of the water, which includes turbidity, color, odor and taste;
2. the chemical quality of the water, which includes organic chemicals and inorganic chemicals;
3. the toxicological characteristics of the water, such as its heavy metal content;
4. the bacteriological characteristics of the water and its micro-organisms;
5. the radioactivity of water.

The physical quality of water

Turbidity describes water which is unclear, where suspended and colloidal particles hinder the passage of light through water. These particles are suspended and can take the form of algae, micro-organisms, dirt, silt, animal or plant matter. It makes sense that drinking this kind of water is undesirable and some form of filtering is highly recommended to remove these partially solid materials.

Color simply refers to the way water is colored by the presence of materials which color it in comparison to its otherwise transparent state. Examples include decaying organic materials from plants, or a high level of mineral trace elements. The blood-like water from Chalice Well in Glastonbury is an example of colored water, producing a rust color due to its high iron content – though in this case the water is therapeutic to drink.

Odor indicates the smell of water. A wide variety of substances can contribute to odor in water. One common odor is chlorine in treated tap water. Try your local swimming pool if you are keen to experience this!

Taste is common to most water unless the water is pure H_2O in the form of distilled water. Common factors contributing to the taste of water are minerals in both inorganic and organic substances.

The chemical quality of water

The chemical quality of water includes organic and inorganic chemicals. Water with a high chemical content can have a harmful effect on the human body. It depends on the quantity of chemicals (parts per million) as well as the varieties of chemicals present.

The toxicological characteristics of water

The toxicology of water depends on the amount of heavy metals in water such as lead, mercury, arsenic, cadmium and selenium. Not all are harmful to human health. Heavy metals such as selenium and chromium are beneficial, depending on quantity, whereas lead and mercury can lead to serious health problems such as brain damage and damage to the central nervous system.

The bacteriological characteristics of water

The bacteriological characteristics of water embrace waterborne bacterial diseases such as cholera, typhoid fever, dysentery, hepatitis and giardia. Common in developing countries including parts of Africa, India, Nepal and South America, these bacterial diseases can have terrible health implications. For the most part, developed countries rarely encounter these waterborne diseases but for anyone who has traveled extensively in developing countries you may have had a first-hand opportunity to experience these bacterial diseases.

The radioactivity of water

It seems odd to add this category to the list as most people are unlikely to encounter water with radioactive contaminants, unless you happen to be drinking contaminated water from uranium mines and nuclear power plants, or drinking water from sources where nuclear bombs are tested or significant radiation has occurred.

Tap water from around the world

With the high level of chemicals found in tap water worldwide, it may not come as a surprise that many of the samples tested in the IHM laboratory resulted in a lack of structured crystal formations. In most cases, the results resembled typical examples of water which reflected negative *hado*, such as water exposed to the words 'I hate you!' or 'dirty'.

I recall my reaction to seeing these images for the first time. Everything I had suspected about the state of our tap water was shown to be true. I rarely drank tap water, but as soon as I saw the following images, my concerns for tap water increased. Like a traveling nomad, these days I choose to carry my own positively-charged *hado* water wherever I go. Whether at a fancy restaurant or on a plane, my *hado* water goes wherever I go.

The following are some examples of tap water from around the world.

In figure 25, we observe a sample of tap water from downtown Los Angeles in the United States. Although it seemed as if the water was trying to form a crystal, from 50 samples tested, figure 25 was the best result.

In figure 26, tap water was taken from Venice, Italy. Venice is considered the water capital of Italy but the water did not render any positive results.

In figure 27, tap water from Paris, France was tested. The blotchy image leads me to believe that, next time I visit Paris, I would prefer to buy a bottle of spring water, just to be on the safe side.

We see in figure 28 that tap water from Asia does not fair any better. Hong Kong tap water shows an improvement, albeit somewhat blurred when compared to positive *hado* water samples. With a population of over 6.9 million, Hong Kong is one of the most densely populated areas in the world, with an overall density of some 6,380 people per square kilometer. It is no wonder the water is having trouble.

When it comes to my home town we see a striking change in water quality. Perth tap water (figure 29) shows a beautiful ice crystal. Not wishing to boast too much about one of the most isolated cities on Earth, the result has a story to it. On one of Masaru Emoto's Australian tours, he presented the results of water samples taken from various cities around Australia that he had visited. He felt that it would be interesting to show tap water from each city so that people attending could see the state of the water where they live.

Some months prior to the tour I was requested to send a sample of Perth tap water to Tokyo for testing. At the time I had no idea what the sample was for, so

I simply collected a sample of tap water from my kitchen sink. I filled a glass bottle and wrapped it in aluminum foil to prevent external information imprinting on the water during transit to IHM in Tokyo. Masaru Emoto showed the picture of Perth tap water during his presentation and it was at this point that I realized that this had been the water from my kitchen sink. Masaru Emoto remarked in his presentation why the water of Perth was so pure.

Driving him back to his hotel after the presentation, I mentioned that perhaps the reason the ice crystal had successfully formed from the otherwise heavily chlorinated tap water, may have been the positive *hado* of our home. I explained that our kitchen faces our meditation room, adorned with several Buddhist paintings and statues, where we conduct daily meditation practice. Upon hearing this, he concluded the reason for the formation of a beautiful ice crystal was due to the *hado* of the home influencing the water. Had I taken water sample from my neighbor's home, the result may not have been the same. This demonstrated to me that, even without intentional human influence, *hado* from the surrounding environment can influence water.

Figure 25. Tap water sample taken from the city of Los Angeles, USA

Figure 26. Tap water sample taken from Venice, Italy. Here the result looks quite beautiful, but nevertheless no ice crystal formed

Bottled water

When we look at the alternatives to tap water the majority of people would consider bottled water as a safe option. However, there is more to this story than meets the eye. Some bottled water is very pure in content and rates highly for vibrational purity, forming strong hexagonal ice crystals when tested. Yet some so-called 'spring' waters available on the market are nothing more than tap water put through a filter to remove the smell and taste of chlorine. Another consideration is where the water traveled before reaching the spring it was drawn from. For example, the water may have traveled through farming areas where the water has been affected by organic or man-made chemicals.

A recent study in the United States conducted by the US Environmental Studies Institute revealed that when 37 different brands of bottled water were tested, only 13 complied with official health standards. This was partly due to the fact that some of the bottled water was simply tap water. The other reasons indicated a lack of pure water sources.

With mineral water the bar is considerably lowered. Unlike tap water, which has to undergo 57 tests for possible contami-

Figure 27. Tap water sample taken from Paris, France

nates, mineral water is tested only for 15 contaminates. To make matters worse, some mineral waters are classified in such a way that they do not even require testing.

The best way to determine what is in your bottled water is to read the labels which, in most cases, will give an indication of the source as well as the mineral content of the water you are purchasing. When we consider than in some cases purchasing a bottle of spring water can be more expensive than purchasing a bottle of beer, it is worth practicing a little consumer discernment at the supermarket.

It is no wonder that, when several bottled waters were tested for ice crystal structure by the researchers at IHM, many did not produce any ice crystals. Some were leading brands of spring water.

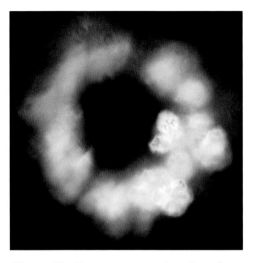

Figure 28. Tap water sample taken from the city of Hong Kong

Figure 29. Tap water sample taken from the author's kitchen sink in Fremantle, Perth, Western Australia

Plastic bottles

I am often asked "What is the best container for water?". I recommend using glass or ceramic water containers. If you choose to use plastic bottles, higher grade plastic is better. Polypropylene plastic is desirable because of its strength and durability. In my opinion, it is better to avoid water bottles which are soft (containing phthalates). The hard plastics often used in water dispensers are a far safer option than the 'squeeze' drink bottles which are so widely available, particularly aimed for children's use.

While re-using plastic bottles is doing a 'good deed' for the environment, recent research indicates that the re-use of plastic bottles may present a potential risk to your health. Dangerous bacteria and potentially toxic plastic compounds have been found in several different types of water bottles in recent studies. Without proper cleaning, re-using plastic bottles can be a health risk that can lead to the ingestion of harmful bacteria. The potential for bacterial contamination also applies to other types of containers such as glass. Sound washing of all water bottles between each use will ensure your water bottle does not become a 'bacteria factory'.

If you want to use a plastic bottle for water storage, conduct the 'sniff' test. This is a direct way to determine whether the container is suitable for water storage. Take any soft plastic water bottle sold in supermarkets, and let your nose do the sniffing. You will soon be able to tell how desirable or undesirable they are. In most cases lifting the lid on soft plastic bottles yields a distinctive chemical cocktail smell. Although there is currently no scientific research linking these soft plastics with carcinogenic agents, let your nose guide you and, ideally, opt for glass or ceramic containers.

Bottled water consumption

In 2004 it was estimated that over 40 billion dollars were made that year from the sale of bottled water. According to a report from the Beverage Marketing Corporation bottled water emerged as the second largest commercial beverage category by volume in the United States, second only to carbonated soft drinks. In the same year the volume of bottled water consumed in USA surpassed 6.8 billion gallons. This translated to an average of 24 gallons per person, and U.S. residents drank more bottled water annually than any other beverage. Today's figures are rising and projected to grow exponentially in the future.

People are prepared to pay top dollar for what is considered good water. The major corporations are jumping on the bandwagon to cash in. Imagine how dramatically the world would change if this same amount of money was invested in cleaning up our water sources and creating sustainable sources of pure water.

Filtered water

The benefit of filtering water has been recognized for thousands of years. Records date back to at least 2000 BC. Some of the early methods of filtering water included digging a hole beside a river or lake and allowing the river sand to filter the water. This simple method is still used today in developing countries. Throughout the ages, particularly with the coming of the industrial age, a variety of filtering methods and filters was invented. Some of these have become the precursors to modern filtration methods.

Filters are composed of substances which absorb, collect or modify contaminants in the water which flows through them. There are several options for filtering water, outlined below, and it is important to research the various methods and products available on the market. It is also important to check the validity of some of the claims made by some distributors of water filters. The water filter business is big business and many extraordinary claims are being made. The use of ice crystal images to endorse water products has become a recent problem, especially as some companies are using the ice crystal images without copyright license to demonstrate the 'before and after' effects of water passed through their filters.

As a rule, the team at IHM has chosen not to endorse one specific water product or water filtration system over another. It is unfair and unwise to use the ice crystal images to position one product over another in the market. IHM has also taken the position that it should not take ice crystal images connected with living individuals such as religious or political figures, since this could taint the value of ice crystal images in the promotion of one belief system or agenda over another. For this reason strict international copyright restrictions are placed on all IHM ice crystal images and the limit of subject content is also restricted.

Common methods of filtering water

Today there are several methods for treating water. Not all are desirable. Some of these methods include:

- Removal of all substances from water, such as reverse osmosis and distillation of water;
- Ozone and ultraviolet sterilization of water, which kills every living thing in water, including both positive and negative substances;
- Activated carbon filters and ceramic candle filters which remove unpleasant taste and odor from water;
- Adding chemicals such as chlorine to water.

Let us now look in greater detail at some of these filtering processes.

Distilled water is a process by which water is either boiled or evaporated and then collected as vapor condensing back into water. Once this process is complete the distilled water is then free of contaminates and minerals, pure H_2O.

Distillation is a slow process and most commercially produced distillers produce at best 1 to 2 litres of distilled water per hour, though the cost of producing distilled water is small. Distillers use little in power consumption and, at less than 10 cents a liter, distillation is very cost effective. Unlike most water filters, distillers will not decrease the quality of water produced (unless the distiller is defective). However, they do require cleaning after each distillation is complete (approximately 4 to 6 liters) as it is necessary to remove substances which did not evaporate in the chamber.

Distilled water has the special ability to actively absorb toxic substances from the body and eliminate them, but drinking distilled water for detoxification should only be used short-term. Longterm use can be dangerous and lead to a rapid loss of electrolytes such as sodium, potassium and chlorides as well as trace minerals such as magnesium. Cooking with distilled water is also not ideal as it draws out beneficial minerals, thus reducing the nutritional value of most foods.

Distilled water is also an active absorber when it comes into contact with air and readily absorbs carbon dioxide, turning the water acidic. Therefore, the more distilled water a person drinks, the greater potential for higher acidity in the body. Curiously, most soft drinks use distilled water as their base. Studies have consistently shown that people who regularly drink large quantities of soft drinks (with or without sugar) lose large amounts of trace minerals into their urine. Loss of minerals without replacement through supplements and correct diet can lead to a risk of osteoporosis, coronary artery disease, high blood pressure and other degenerative diseases. There is also a direct correlation between drinking distilled water and cardiovascular disease. The longer one drinks distilled water the more one is susceptible to mineral deficiencies.

Unless you are drinking distilled water for the purpose of detoxifying the body (for no more than 21 days) as part of a well balanced diet, without combining it with fasting, the benefits are real. But longterm use is not considered to be good for your body and general health.

It should be mentioned here that distilled water is used by the researchers at IHM for ice crystal experiments due to its pure water qualities. It provides a blank surface on which to imprint water with information.

Reverse Osmosis is a process whereby water is forced under high pressure through an ultra-fine, semi-permeable membrane designed to allow individual water molecules through whilst rejecting contaminates. The membrane acts as a filter removing most harmful compounds. Although not as effective in purification as distilled water, reverse osmosis is perhaps the closest purified water to distilled water.

Once the contaminants are separated from water, they are washed away to prevent buildup in the purifier. Reverse osmosis removes a wide range of contaminants including turbidity, colloidal matter, dissolved solids, pesticides, herbicides and toxic metals. Like distillation, reverse osmosis is a slow process, usually carried out drop by drop, and it takes 2-3 liters to produce one liter of reverse osmosis water.

Similar to distilled water, reverse osmosis water is considered 'blank' or 'dead' water which retains minimal trace minerals beneficial for the body. As with distilled water, it is not recommended for longterm consumption as it leaches the body's minerals.

Activated carbon filters are very effective for removing pollutants to improve the taste of water as well as to remove color and odor. Compared with reverse osmosis and distilled water, carbon filters are super-fast in delivering clean water for safe consumption.

Activated carbon filters are often made from coal, coconut, lignite, wood or a combination of these. When these substances are subjected to high temperatures in the absence of oxygen, millions of microscopic pores are produced which have an excellent capacity to remove an array of contaminates.

Carbon filters usually come in two varieties: block or granulated. Block filters are superior to granulated filters, provided they are well constructed, allowing water to move slowly through the filter. This method is more desirable since it allows a higher quantity of impurities to be absorbed. Most carbon filters have a life of 6 months to 1 or 2 years depending upon the make and model, before one is required to change the filter.

A *ceramic candle filter* is a hollow core of unglazed porcelain, which is very effective in removing impurities. Most ceramic candle filters become discolored with regular use, so it is necessary to clean them regularly with a soft brush or fine abrasor to remove the buildup of grime. Many ceramic filters also combine carbon filters to increase their effectiveness and odor-reducing qualities.

Energizing water

It is well known that water carries information. Unfortunately this includes electromagnetic waves acting negatively and constituting energy-pollution. It is not sufficient to remove the physical contaminates in water. The vibratory information of harmful substances such as heavy metals remain and are transmitted to humans when consumed. These vibrations impact on the body because the vibrationally-contaminated water searches through the water in the body to find balance.

Although many people are now taking steps to remove the harmful chemicals in tap water, few people realize that drinking vibrationally-negative water is harmful. This is water with a negative *hado* charge. Negatively-charged water is full of energetically foreign substances and frequencies that leach vital energy from our body.

Negatively-charged water is often full of the effects of electromagnetic radiation, mostly man-made, reducing its capacity to hold ions within its unbalanced structure. This 'dead' water is disorganized and, as it lacks a natural structure, it forms disfigured ice crystals or none at all. We can observe this in the tap water samples taken from most major cities worldwide or in water which as been exposed to negative stimuli.

The solution is to energize water. This process can be as simple as charging water with positive thoughts, words, images and intention. As we have seen, one of the most powerful affirmations to charge and recover water is to bless the water with the words 'love and gratitude'. As simple as it sounds, the power of our positive intention can have a dramatic effect on water at the molecular level.

Energized water can erase the memory of harmful substances which have been stored previously. It recovers the water to a balanced state in accordance with a more natural order. When we speak about the quality of water we need to also consider the energetic quality of water. Energizing water allows it to become 'alive', and this has numerous benefits for all those who drink it.

Some of the benefits of drinking energized water include the following:

- Energized water is super-absorbent for the body;
- It fully hydrates the body;
- It detoxifies contaminants in the body;
- It boosts the body's immune system;
- It is a wonderful anti-oxidant, collecting free radicals;
- It assists the body in eliminating toxins, and cell and organ rejuvenation is also accelerated;
- Energized water assists in generating alkaline over acidic toxins in the body;

- It is the best carrier of beneficial minerals;
- It absorbs more nutrients than regular tap water and is beneficial for those who experience skin irritations caused by showering in chlorinated water;
- Energized water is softer and has less surface tension, which means you require less detergent when washing clothes.

What is the best water to drink?

I am often asked what I consider to be the best water to drink. In my experience the best water is free of contaminants, it has been re-mineralized and it has been imbued with positive *hado*. If you begin with water from a natural, reliable source which is free from contaminates, such as a natural spring, high in minerals and possessing good natural *hado*, drink this and lots of it. If you cannot get access to natural water I recommend the following three-stage process:

Stage 1. *Remove the impurities and contaminants.* To use tap water, we first need to purify the water of contaminants such as chlorine, trihalomethanes, organic chemicals, polyaromatic hydrocarbons, lead, aluminum, cadmium, and fluoride. A good carbon water filter will achieve this result. Once we have removed these contaminants the water requires re-mineralization.

Stage 2. *Re-mineralizing water.* There are now many water filter products on the market which remove contaminates as well as re-mineralizing water. By adding useful minerals back into water, the water absorbs the natural minerals the body needs. These are minerals we would normally receive if we were drinking water from a pure source. Store your purified water in a glass or ceramic vessel and add mineral stones which can be purchased over the internet or from health stores who sell quality water filters.

Stage 3. *Energize the water.* Once the water is re-mineralized, the water should then be energized. Energized water removes electromagnetic waves which can otherwise disrupt our energy systems. Energized water cancels negative imprints, replacing them with positive imprints. A simple heartfelt water blessing will suffice. One way is to place a love and gratitude coaster under the water overnight (these are available from www.hado.net). This will mirror a positive effect to the water, imbuing it with the positive *hado* of the ice crystal of love and gratitude.

Of course, the greater the positive human interaction, the greater the energizing effect. Chapter 8 suggests a simple meditation practice which anyone can use to imbue water with positive *hado*. You can actually taste the difference. It is a simple water blessing exercise which produces remarkable results even in ordinary tap water.

When blessing water, remember to 'thank' the water and appreciate it when you drink it. Knowing that water it is a precious gift, one should contemplate this with a feeling of gratitude. The more consciously you drink water, the more that water will give back to you in terms of health, vitality and longevity.

CHAPTER 4

HEXAGONAL WATER

In ice crystals, the hexagon is one of the hallmarks of quality, purity and positive *hado*. It can be readily observed in the structure of positively-charged water. Water which has been exposed to positive influences or water which has a natural, pure order exhibits a hexagonal structure.

Extensive research on the positive and life-giving effects of hexagonally structured water has been conducted in Asia by scientific researchers such as Dr Mu Shik Jhon and Dr Yang H Oh. Through their and others' research, tremendous discoveries have been made which are slowly becoming recognized throughout the wider scientific community.

Figure 30. Underground water from North Island, New Zealand

Their research demonstrates the correlation between hexagonal structure and wellness. The work of Masaru Emoto also illustrates this point. The benefits of drinking hexagonally structured water is beneficial on many levels, including heightened immune function, weight loss, better hydration, better absorption of nutrients in the body, increased longevity and an increase in cell production.

One interesting finding from Dr Mu Shik Jhon is in the area of snow water. He found that water which is super-cooled, such as snow water, has greater hexagonal structure. When such water becomes frozen the hexagonal structure increases. Pure sources of water, such as those found in mountainous regions and underground sources, favor hexagonal formations. Underground water sampled in New Zealand produces a fine example of hexagonal structure – see figure 30.

Snow water which freezes under super-cooled conditions in the atmosphere produces a high hexagonal structure. It has also been observed that recipients of snow water, such as plant life and other organisms, experience an increase in physiological responses. If plants grow better and become more resilient after receiving snow water, would the same be the case for human beings? The answer is 'yes', but to go and acquire vast quantities of snow water for daily consumption is, for most people, not possible. However, there are some brands of snow water which are available on the market for consumers and, in cases where genuine water sources are drawn for commercial use, it is not necessary to drink super-cold water because the hexagonal information continues to be carried when the water is consumed at room temperature. Water also has the ability to carry hexagonal information even when it is taken into the body. Although the temperature of the water increases, the hexagonal structure and vibrational signature remain.

Water also retains its hexagonal structure if it has a high content of certain minerals. There is a correlation between springwater which has a high content of minerals such as magnesium, sodium, potassium, calcium and sulphide ions, and hexagonal structure. When drinking springwater with a high mineral content one not only receives the benefit of drinking hexagonally structured water, but also one receives beneficial minerals the body needs.

It makes sense that drinking positively-charged water will give us added benefits to our health. So how do we make hexagonally structured water? Essentially, there are four main methods.

The first is to obtain super-cooled water such as snow water, or water which has been cooled to between -30 and -40°C. For the most part this will be hard for most people unless you have access to water from mountainous regions or happen to live in such areas.

The second is to obtain water with a high mineral content. Water with high calcium content has been determined to generate the most hexagon-forming structure of all minerals found in springwater.

The third is to use ionization or strong magnetic fields, as is the case with vortex machines. Water exposed to ionization or magnetic fields becomes slightly alkaline and, consequently, hexagonally structured. Spiral movement is a constant in all living systems. We see this in the natural flow of water in rivers and streams. It is also present in the human circulatory system. In nature these vortices occur naturally, acting as powerful resonance structures which energize, purify and electrify water as it moves. Vortex machines recreate these qualities to form water which is energized, oxygenated and hexagonally structured. Today, there are several products on the market which produce hexagonal structure with ionization. As with all methods of increasing the hexagonal structure of water, one should do some research to determine which method best suits your needs.

The fourth and easiest way, illustrated through ice crystal photography, is to use consciousness. If we imbue water with positive information – such as playing positive music to water, exposing it to stimuli such as positive words, images and the like, we increase the vibratory level and thus the hexagonal structure too.

Hydration

Many forms of water are composed of relatively large water conglomerates which are too large to move freely in the cells of the human body. This water must be reorganized within the body to penetrate the cells. The smaller molecular structure of hexagonal water allows for faster transmission through cellular membranes. This has been verified using bio-electrical impedance analysis (BIA).

Many alternative practitioners now use bio-electrical impedance analysis and a variety of other methods to assess the level of health in their patients. According to one practitioner, Dr Donald Mayfield, there is no question that hexagonally-structured water provides more rapid hydration. He writes: "Hexagonal water helps to improve a number of measurable parameters in the human body. In my experience, even though many of my patients are drinking the recommended amount of daily water, they are still dehydrated. Hexagonally-structured water hydrates the body more rapidly by encouraging faster water uptake. I have been able to observe that the intracellular and extracellular water ratio begins to normalize within 10-15 minutes… Because of its link to so many functions, hexagonal water also appears to 'jump-start' numerous bodily functions – even to enhance the water-protein communication network in the body."

Most disease can be traced to dehydration. It is the number one cause of stress in the human body. It has been determined that, with high consumption of carbonated and caffeinated soft drinks as well as coffee, the vast majority of the population in developed countries are dehydrated. Even those who do not drink such things may lack the quality of water that the body will recognize for adequate hydration. Many soft drinks also use distilled water as a base, which aids in removing essential minerals from the body. When there is insufficient water, every biological function suffers. Chronic dehydration has also been linked with headaches, asthma, constipation, weight gain, edema (water retention), colitis, diabetes, heartburn, chronic fatigue, peptic ulcer pain, high blood pressure, blood cholesterol and many other symptoms. Recent research reveals that it is not just the lack of water, but the lack of hexagonally-structured water that is of greatest importance.

Hexagonal water is assimilated more easily at the cellular level. It may be one of the best ways to overcome dehydration and protect your body from the symptoms of disease and premature aging. According to Dr Mu Shik Jhon,

"Replenishing the hexagonal water in our bodies can increase vitality, slow the aging process and prevent disease."

Water is a network of hydrogen-bonded molecules. It can form numerous structures, depending on how individual molecules bond together. One of these structures is the hexagon – composed of six water molecules. Hexagonal water forms an organized crystalline matrix with properties that are different from ordinary water. Hexagonal water appears to play an important role in biological functions. It is being linked with improved hydration, enhanced nutrient absorption, DNA function and improvements in metabolic efficiency.

The average adult is roughly 70% water. Our brain is made up of 74% water, our blood is as high as 82% and our kidneys are 82% water. Our denser bones are 22% and our muscles 75% water. With all this water in our body it is easy to appreciate how important it is and how dependant we are upon it.

The secret of youth

The amount of hexagonal water in the body has even been correlated with aging. From a cellular level, the older we are the less water we have. A fertilized egg is over 95% water, a child 80%, a grown adult is 70% and a elderly person is as little as 60% water. As we age the movement of water in and out of cells slows. Cells function at their best when 60% of the total body's water is inside cells, but aging brings a decrease in water and thus less water in and out of cells, often measuring as low as 40%. With a decrease of water content, cells have less of an ability to re-hydrate.

Hexagonal water also appears to increase cellular hydration more rapidly, delivering more nutrients and removing more wastes from the body than non-hexagonally structured water. This has been observed by Dr Seiji Katayama using magnetic resonance imaging (MRI).

The amount of water we have corresponds to vitality. One way to check if you are hydrated is to press your finger into the center of your palm. Hold down in one place for about ten seconds. As soon as you release your finger, the skin should immediately spring back to its original shape. This indicates good hydration. If the skin returns slowly or a dent is left for more than a second or two, go and drink a few glasses of pure water, since your body is sending you a clear message.

You can readily observe how, as a person ages, they retain less water. The skin begins to lose its elastic quality, the face becomes wrinkled and certain parts begin to sag. Unfortunately, getting old never goes out of fashion and happens to everyone, but one of the secrets to youth is good hydration. Vitality equals hydration. So in order to maintain a more youthful appearance, make drinking positively charged water a priority – it's a lot more effective than cosmetics and far less expensive.

The hexagon in nature

The hexagon is not only a feature of pure water it has also been adopted by nature and, in particular, the humble honey bee. Honey bees have been making honey for thousands of years, and there are millions of different shapes they could have chosen for their honeycombs. So why are honeycombs shaped hexagonally? One reason is efficient packing: to be as efficient as possible, individual honeycomb cells should tessellate perfectly so there are no gaps. Tessellating shapes are the most efficient way to pack, enabling the most cells in the least amount of space. This enables bees to store the maximum amount of honey in hexagonally structured cells.

If cells were round and formed into a lattice network, the number of round cells surrounding one central cell would be a group of six. However, if utilizing round cells, there would be a lot of wasted space which the bees would have to fill with wax. A hexagonally structured matrix enables greater efficiency, with no gaps. With a perfectly fitting lattice, dirt and predators are not able to enter the honeycomb and the structure is therefore safer and stronger.

Hexagons also correspond closely to the shape of bees, and the closer packed the bees are, the greater the benefit of accumulated body heat, making a hive more efficient. The hexagon provides the maximum space using the least amount of material. This means it can store a lot of honey whilst being economical on beeswax. The way a hexagon encloses an area into equal parts with the least perimeter and wastage is called the Honeycomb Conjecture.

It should also be noted that honey never spoils. There is no need to refrigerate it and it can be stored unopened, indefinitely, at room temperature. Honey is also one of the oldest foods in existence. It was found in the tomb of the Egyptian pharaoh Tutankhamun and was still edible when found. Honey is considered a divine elixir and has been used for centuries for its curative and divine qualities. Could there be a connection between the purity of honey stored within a hexagonal structure and the hexagonal structure of pure water?

A common misconception is that snowflakes are frozen raindrops. Sometimes raindrops do freeze as they fall, but this is called sleet. Sleet particles do not have the elaborate and symmetrical patterning found in snowflakes. Snowflakes are formed when water vapor condenses directly into ice, from gaseous to solid form. This process happens in the clouds themselves. The patterns which subsequently emerge form as the crystals grow.

When snowflakes are very small, they are mostly simple hexagonal prisms. But as they grow, branches sprout from the corners to make more complex shapes, often displaying branching structures. This parallels what occurs in ice crystal photography when water is exposed to positive stimuli.

What have honey and snowflakes to do with ice crystals? The answer lies in the correlation between the divine order of nature and our consciousness. If positive intention can create hexagonally structured water and bees store honey in honeycombs, this suggests a kind of perfect form which expresses the divine or the principle of creation in manifestation. This divinity is present when positive *hado* is present. The correlation between the hexagon (the basis of positive *hado*) is explored in the following section on the sacred geometry of the hexagon.

The sacred geometry of the hexagon

We know about the importance of the hexagon in water in relationship to purity and natural sources. We also know its importance with regards to positive *hado*, but what of the link between the shape of the hexagon and symbology? This question concerns the symbology of the union of the sacred opposites. Symbols are the language of the unconscious, and we use them daily and live our lives by them, whether or not we are aware of this. The Yin and Yang symbol ☯ represents a perfect balance of opposites, demonstrating how Yin, the feminine principle, resides within Yang, the masculine principle, and Yang within Yin. As we see in figure 31, when water was exposed to the Yin-Yang symbol ☯ the ice crystal closely resembled the shape of the symbol.

Figure 31. Water shown the symbol for Yin and Yang

Another symbol which represents the union of opposites, pointing to the hexagon in ice crystals, is the Jewish symbol of the Star of David ✡. The name David in ancient Hebrew (during the time of king David) is made up of the three letters *Dalet*, *Vav* and *Dalet* again. *Dalet* in ancient Hebrew actually means 'triangle', but the two triangles interlaced in the star reveal a far deeper meaning. Figure 32 shows the ice crystal which formed when water was shown the Star of

David symbol. When looking at the center of the ice crystal one can clearly see the symbol for the Star of David as well as the hexagon at its center.

Figure 32. Water shown the symbol of the Star of David

Throughout several cultures the symbolism of purity and balance has been represented by the union of opposites. The male symbol is an upwards pointing triangle △ and the female symbol is a downwards pointing triangle ▽. When these two symbols are joined they form the Star of David and as we have already discussed, this union forms at its center a hexagon. We will now delve deeper into the symbology of this union, exploring the opposite qualities and the correlation between this union and the symbology of the hexagon.

The male symbol is associated with the male organ or phallus. In ancient times, all things resembling this symbol were revered, such as mountains, pointed rocks and later the spear, the blade, the obelisk and the pyramid. The symbol of the male was also embodied and revered throughout indigenous cultures in the form of the 'Sky Father' and 'Grandfather Sun'. The Sun represented the procreative power of the male principle. The rays of the Sun shone upon the Earth, impregnating her with light which gave birth to and supported life. The Sun is also synonymous with the eastern direction, a symbol of birth and renewal. With the dawn of the new day, the Sun brings light into a world of darkness. Even today the symbol of the male principle is alive and erect. We need look no further than our cities where great men have constructed upstanding skyscrapers and monuments designed to impress. In some respects, not a great deal has changed over the centuries.

The female symbol is of a vessel, a down-turned triangle representing the female genitalia. This symbol was used in ancient times and revered in natural formations such as caves, grottoes, bodies of water, crevasses, cracks in rocks, openings in the trunk of a mighty tree – all synonyms with the sacred orifice of the divine feminine. Even the ocean is considered by seafarers as 'she'. The female symbol is also represented by the chalice, grail or cup. In Native American traditions the Earth was considered a mother and the Moon a grandmother.

In post-Constantine Christianity the snake became wrongly associated with the Devil, women became regarded as inherently evil and the left hand was dirty and unclean. Yet the snake is a symbol of intuitive wisdom, and the left-hand side of the body corresponds to the right hemisphere of the brain – a union of opposites – which science tell us is directly associated with creativity, inspirations, artistic qualities and intuition. The role of women as half of the human race needs no argument.

Although both symbols of male and female are unique and celebrated in their own right, it is the union of these divine opposites which creates all forms. This union of opposites is known as the *Hieros Gamos*, the sacred bride and bridegroom. In many ancient cultures this mystical union is revered in the shape of the hexagram or hexagon. The *Hieros Gamos* wedding represents the cosmic dance of opposites. When the harmonious play of positive and negative forces are joined, wellbeing, fertility, creativity and wholeness are created. It is any

Figure 33. *Thanka* (Buddhist painting) of Chakrasamvara, representing inner union

wonder that, when ice crystals are exposed to positive impressions or formed in accord with the purity of nature, the union of opposites, the male △ and the female ▽ form the Star of David ✡ and, at the core, a hexagon is formed.

In Buddhism, the divine opposites are celebrated as wisdom and compassion. Wisdom is associated with the feminine and compassion with the masculine. In Buddhist *thankas* (Tibetan religious paintings used in meditation) this divine union is depicted as Buddhas in union. Unlike Hindu Tantra, where the emphasis is on outer union and sexual embrace, the meaning from the Buddhist Tantric perspective is that of blending one's mind with the perfection of wisdom and compassion, as illustrated in figure 33 showing Chakrasamvara, a deity who represents the highest joy arising from Tantric practice. Tantric Buddhism makes use of the yogic practices of visualization, mantra, mudra, mandalas and symbolic ritual. In the case of Chakrasamvara, the male deity represents active compassion and the female form represents all-pervading wisdom. Their union symbolizes the inner union of the meditator who has gone beyond duality and has achieved highest bliss which comes as a result of this practice.

When water as shown the words 'Wisdom and Compassion' (figure 34) it formed two crystals, one holding the other. In this case, wisdom supports compassion, the feminine supporting the masculine and clearly not the other way around!

When I began studying ice crystal photography I immediately noticed the hexagonal structure and, through further research, saw the connection between the union of opposites. Since the dawn of time human beings have intuitively aligned with the divine laws of nature and the hexagon, and purity and perfect balance have been reflected through symbology as well as in nature.

When ice crystals are exposed to positive vibrations the very nature of reality is revealed – a hidden message for all of us.

The number six

When we examine the significance of the hexagon appearing in ice crystal formations it is worth noting the numerology and metaphysical qualities of the

Figure 34. Water shown the words 'Wisdom and Compassion'

number six and how this relates to the hexagon from an esoteric perspective. The number six represents family and symbolizes the home. It represents domestic bliss, responsibility, compassion, marriage and devotion. Six is also associated with parenthood, healers and counselors. It includes the fraternity or brotherhood and the sorority or sisterhood. It is the common bond of closeness between people, representing love, nurturing, harmony, mutual support and justice.

The number six is traditionally a number of perfection and marriage. It is the product of the feminine number two and the masculine number three. In the Bible, the world was created in six days. Six is the perfection of balance and reflection. When observing this in ice crystals, it is no wonder that the six-sided hexagonal structure features so strongly.

The root of the word 'hexagon' comes from Greek *Hexad*, which means the quality of 'sixness'. A Greek philosopher once said "Number is within all things." The hexagon is often a subconscious reminder of perfection and intelligent design. Whether we recognize this consciously or not, the hexagon is an antidote to chaos in our times.

The Greek mathematical philosophers called six the 'perfection of parts', because six is the only number that is both the sum and the product of the same three numbers. That is, $1 + 2 + 3 = 6$ and also $1 \times 2 \times 3 = 6$.

The numbers that six can be divided by (the divisors 1, 2 and 3) are the only set of numbers where each number is a divisor of the other two. Six is the only number other than the number ten that can be formed by the multiplication of two divisors other than 1. For example: $6 = 2 \times 3$ whereas $10 = 2 \times 5$.

Mathematics is universally respected as a primary source of objective truth, and it is concerned with number and form. But how do these mathematical properties translate into the world around us and why is the number six considered the materialization of perfection? Six is the first perfect number. Returning to our friends the bees, a honeycomb vessel with six sides holds the most honey with the minimum effort and use of materials. In industry, hexagonal structures are used in storage systems because they are the most efficient way of using space.

The electronics industry also utilizes the qualities of the hexagon. Silicon atoms of quartz are arranged in hexagons and the piezoelectric nature of quartz means pressure yields electricity and electric currents yield regular mechanical pulses. This enables the functioning of the quartz watch. So, even in the most modern of uses, the hexagon and 'sixness' are associated with material per-fection. Six is also the perfect divider of the circle, and the radius of a circle divides its circumference into six points, forming once again a perfect hexagon.

Six is a mystic number represented in nature by ice crystals, honeycombs, snow crystals and the petals of many flowers. Associations with the number six vary according to tradition and religious belief, but they can carry a similar theme: in the Bible, the world was created in six days, in Jewish tradition creation took six thousand years, and in China the number six is designated as the number of Heaven.

However, the Serpent, associated with the Devil, was created on the sixth day, and the number 666 is that of the Anti-Christ – when you add up the numbers corresponding to the Greek letters for Anti-Christ, they add up to 666. While Christianity has lost the concept of balance between opposites, it is nevertheless demonstrated in the numerology associated with the Serpent and the Anti-Christ, which serve as the antithesis of God, goodness and the Christ.

When we look at ice crystal formed from water exposed to the number 666 (figure 35), a distorted crystal is the result. However this crystal was selected by Masaru Emoto because it has an almost attractive quality – an ice crystal which seems half good and half bad. Perhaps water is telling us that even the 'Beast' seeks happiness and wholeness.

Figure 35. Water shown the numbers 666

Since the dawn of time water has been revered as a symbol of purity and a giver of life. Our ancestors made shrines in watery places, to honor water for its life-giving properties. When water is fertilized by sunlight, using soil as a substrate, it provides the impetus for birth and life.

The cleansing properties of water

Water cleans the body and purifies it. These two qualities confer a highly symbolic, even sacred status to water. Water is therefore a key element in ceremonies and religious rites. Not only does water wash away external signs of dirtiness, but also it erases spiritual difficulties. Through contact with or immersion in water, believers can cleanse themselves of wrong-doing or profanity, or simply rid themselves of the signs of the secular world and prepare themselves to enter the religious and spiritual realm. Ablutions before prayer, weddings, or other ceremonies are common across the world.

Spiritual associations with water can occur in various ways, depending on the culture and the objective. In Christianity, immersion in water is seen as a symbolic rebirth wherein the believer is cleansed of all sins through the power of Jesus Christ (who is called 'the living water' in the Bible). In Hinduism water is used to cleanse, all water is held to be sacred, and holy places are often located on the banks of rivers, which are viewed as particularly sacred.

Although water is intrinsically linked to life, vitality and fertility, it is also intimately linked to death. The absence of water kills as fast as any disease. Even when communities are prepared for natural disasters, floods, droughts, famines, and landslides can still wreak havoc. Water brings both life and death, and it is fitting that water is a common element in the death rites of cultures across the planet.

In many cultures, water is used not only to purify the dead body in preparation for the afterlife, but also to cleanse those who have come in contact with the body, in preparation for their own rebirth into the land of the living after having had contact with the land of the dead.

From the earliest times, healing cults have been associated with water sources. In Europe of the Neolithic period and the Bronze Age, religious worship took place at numerous springs. Linked to water's purifying element is the belief in water's intrinsic healing and protection properties. Used in blessing, naming and christening ceremonies, water is sprinkled around an abode or daubed on the forehead, to protect a household or a person from danger or evil.

Water's healing properties are sometimes thought to be an inherent supernatural power of water. In medieval times many Christians hung an amulet filled with holy water at the entrance to their house to prevent evil spirits from entering.

Washing in sacred waters is accepted to provide healing from illness, ranging from arthritis to blindness, and pilgrims have traveled the world over to immerse themselves in healing waters. At Lourdes in France, millions of people gather to bathe in or collect some of the water from hot springs said to have healing properties. Over the decades, hundreds of miracles have been reported, 67 of which have been officially recognized by the Roman Catholic Church.

Water is not seen only as a bringer of life, but also as a destructive force to be reckoned with. With creation stories come stories of destruction. Nearly all cultures have some version of the great flood story, which wiped out former peoples who were deemed in some way to have disappointed the gods. In these stories, acts of contrition by humans, or of forgiveness by deities, avoids total extinction.

The religious relationship with water

Virtually all cultures have formed a mythology around water. It features in the first chapter of the Bible: "The Spirit of God hovered over the face of the waters" (Genesis 1:2), "The earth was founded upon the waters" (Genesis 1:6-7, 9-10) and "God commanded the water to bring out an abundance of living souls" (Genesis 1:20-21).

The common belief throughout the Old Testament is that water was a mystically powerful element which, being connected with God, could cleanse sins and defilements, renewing the human being. Water has taken on the religious symbolism of life. Christ said that water was the means to spiritual rebirth into the kingdom of heaven. It took on the symbolism of spiritual grace: while water purified the body, the Spirit cleansed the soul, thus connecting the cleansing of washing in water with the bathing of the soul in the waters of Spirit.

In Islam water is important too. Muslims must be ritually pure before approaching God in prayer. Some mosques have a courtyard with a pool of clear water in the center or a fountain, but in most mosques the ablutions are done out-side the walls. The Qa'aba in Mecca is located directly above an ancient sacred spring. Of course, being a faith originating in the Arabian desert, water takes on extra meaning since dusty dryness is most people's normal condition and cleans-ing in water is thereby an exceptional circumstance akin to spiritual cleansing.

In Hinduism water has a special place. To Hindus all water is sacred, especially rivers, and there are seven sacred rivers, namely the Ganges, Yamuna, Godavari, Sarasvati, Narmada, Sindhu and Kaveri. Although Hinduism encompasses many different shades of belief, what unites them all is a striving to attain purity and avoid the defiling pollution of mundane or unwholesome acts, physically and spiritually.

In Buddhism, water is one of the traditional offerings made upon shrines. The first offering is water for cleansing and the second is water for drinking. In Buddhist funerals water is poured into a bowl placed before the monks and the one who has died.

In Judaism ritual washing restores or maintains ritual purity. These ablutions involve washing the hands, or the hands and the feet, or total immersion in 'living water' such as the sea, a river or a spring. The ritual washing of hands is performed before and after meals and on many other occasions.

Shinto, Japan's indigenous religion, is based on the veneration of the *kami*, the innumerable deities believed to inhabit mountains, trees, rocks, springs and other natural phenomena. Waterfalls are held sacred and standing under them is believed to purify all negative impurities.

In Chinese temples some traditions feature ponds with bridges crossing them in a zigzag pattern. These bridges prevent ghosts from crossing since, according to *feng shui* tradition, they can cross water only in a straight line.

When the Romans invaded Celtic lands in France, Germany and Britain, they often saw a golden glitter in the lakes and rivers. Upon closer examination they found that coins and bracelets were thrown into the lakes and rivers to appease and thank the Celtic gods who were believed to live in the water.

Water has always been celebrated throughout the world as a precious substance bestowing purification and cleansing. We will now look at some of the ice crystal results from healing wells and springs tested for purity by IHM.

Healing Water

Springwater is commonly reported to have healing qualities, worldwide. Masaru Emoto was drawn to test healing springs in an effort to quantify the healing effects of these waters.

Chalice Well, Glastonbury, UK

There are many myths associated with Glastonbury, including those of the Holy Grail and King Arthur. With regards to Chalice Well the story of Joseph of Arimathea is of particular interest.

Joseph of Arimathea was the Biblical figure who took the body of Jesus off the cross after the crucifixion. After the crucifixion Joseph was forced to flee from Palestine, and after much travail he came to Britain with a number of followers. As the story goes, he brought with him the Holy Grail, the cup used by Jesus at the Last Supper. Some versions have it that he brought two vials filled with the blood and sweat of Jesus, captured from Jesus' side when he was wounded on the cross.

When Joseph came to Britain he was granted land at Glastonbury by the local druid-king. On his arrival at Glastonbury, Joseph had stuck his thorn staff in the earth, whereupon it formed roots and grew branches, leaves and flowers. Descendants of his staff survive today on Wearyall Hill and in the grounds of the later Glastonbury Abbey, where they continue to bloom to this day at the original Christmas (twelve days after our present-day Christmas). The Glastonbury Thorn is a variety native to Lebanon.

Joseph is said to have established the first church in England at Glastonbury. As to the whereabouts of the Holy Grail, its location remains a mystery. Some legends have it that Joseph buried the Grail at the foot of Glastonbury Tor, whereupon a spring of blood gushed forth from the ground. At the base of the Tor is Chalice Well. The water that issues forth has a reddish tinge due to the high iron content of the water. Some years ago I had the opportunity to visit Chalice Well and taste the water. It had a strong mineral taste and its vibrational quality could not have been more striking. You can feel the water washing through your body – a sign of its being structured water.

When a water sample from Chalice Well was placed under the microscope by IHM's researchers, it produced a beautiful ice crystal as seen in figure 36.

Figure 36. Ice crystal from water of Chalice Well

Trevi Fountain, Rome, Italy

The Trevi Fountain is one of the world's most photographed monuments in Rome, and many would agree that, among the many wonderful buildings of Baroque Rome, the Trevi Fountain is unrivalled as a spectacular aquatic structure. See figure 37.

There are many legends regarding the Trevi Fountain. In 19 BC Marco Vespasiano Agrippa decided to construct a long canal to feed the springs he developed near the Pantheon in Rome. The legend states that soldiers were sent to search for water springs close to Rome and, during their search, met a young

Figure 37. Trevi Fountain in Rome, Italy

girl who led them to the pure springs. It is from this legend that the aqueduct received its name as the Virgin Water aqueduct.

During the times of antiquity, a glass of the fresh water from the Trevi Fountain was said to ensure good fortune and a rapid return to Rome. Over the course of time, this practice was replaced by the tossing of a coin in the fountain. The tradition calls for one to throw the coin over one's left shoulder while standing with one's back to the fountain. The Trevi Fountain today contains a varied collection of international coins tossed by travelers wishing to return to this distinctly romantic and wonderful place. There is a second romantic ritual associated with the Trevi

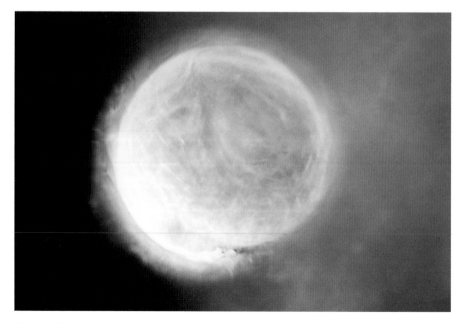

Figure 38. Ice crystal from water collected from the Trevi Fountain

Fountain, pertaining to the miniature fountain on the left side known as 'the small fountain of lovers'. According to the legend, couples that drink from the smaller fountain will forever be faithful to their partner and, as a result, this attracts millions of visitors each year.

Trevi Fountain in Rome produced an amazing ice crystal, as seen in figure 38. Unlike any other ice crystal, the result appears like a radiant sphere which looks almost like a planet from space. Perhaps the water is showing all of the coins which have been thrown into the fountain over the years. During a visit to Trevi Fountain my wife and I added a few coins and drank from the small fountain of lovers. The results appear to be working still to this day!

Lourdes, France

The 'fountain of miracles' is visited by more than four million people each year. In 1858, a fourteen year old peasant girl named Bernadette Soubirous had a

Figure 39. Ice crystal from a water sample from Lourdes, France

series of eighteen visions of the Virgin Mary, who appeared in a niche in the grotto of Massabielle near Lourdes. During her ninth apparition, on 25 February 1858, Bernadette claimed to have been directed to a then-undiscovered spring in the grotto. The discovery by Bernadette was witnessed by hundreds of onlookers, and was eventually declared a miraculous event.

Later studies have shown that the water of Lourdes is pure, containing chlorides of soda, lime and magnesia, bicarbonates of lime and magnesia, silicates of lime and aluminum, oxide of iron, sulphate of soda, and phosphate. Yet despite the material substances it is the vibrational quality of the water which is most apparent. The positive *hado* of the water is indicated by the number of miracles associated with this important spring.

A frozen water sample taken from this spring was put under the microscope by a researcher at IHM and produced a beautiful ice crystal (see figure 39). The ice crystal from Lourdes resembles the collective wishes of those who seek to be spiritually cleansed by the spring's healing waters. The ice crystal suggests a circle of protection and love, much like a mother has for her child. This ice crystal reveals the holiness and purity of this special place.

CHAPTER 5

HOW OUR CONSCIOUSNESS AFFECTS WATER

Our consciousness has a real ability to affect water – so much so that we can observe before- and after-effects with dramatic results. With our words or thoughts we can change water's structure from disfigured to beautiful formations. But how does this occur?

The answer lies in our ability to raise the vibratory level of water through interacting with it. Our *hado* can be used to increase the vibratory level of water, to revive its natural order and hexagonal structure. The same is true of negative *hado*. Water which has a natural hexagonal structure can be destroyed by our negative thoughts, words or intention. Either way, we have an ability to affect water.

Play music with words of anger and hatred, and beautiful ice crystals become diminished and lose their structure. Play uplifting music with words of love and thanks, and the water will recover to a natural, harmonious state. This is true for a small or large body of water – however the lasting impact is determined by the power and purity of this intention. Masaru Emoto has conducted several experiments in Europe and the United States where hundreds of people gathered with the clear intention to bless a large body of water. In all cases, when the water was tested, the results were beautiful ice crystals where previously they were not present prior to the blessing.

Positive interaction with water increases its positive *hado*. Negative interaction diminishes water. This is not too dissimilar to ourselves. When we are spoken to pleasantly we feel good, and when we are shouted at with words of anger, we feel bad. The water in our bodies responds, whatever the influence.

The spirit of words

Just as we human beings hold specific vibrations, so do words. What gives a word a meaning are two primary factors. The first factor is the vibration of the word itself. The second is the interaction of this vibration with the observer.

Every word has an intrinsic vibration, a frequency which can suggest harmony, discord or somewhere in between. It is interesting to note that this intrinsic vibration remains the same regardless of language. The phrase 'thank you' produces beautifully structured ice crystals in any language (figures 8 and 9). The vibration that comes from words will produce either balanced or disfigured ice crystals, depending on the *hado* of the word. When observed under the microscope, water which has been shown the word 'dirty' produces an ice crystal which indeed looks dirty, whereas water shown the word 'cleanliness' produces a beautifully balanced ice crystal (figures 40 and 41).

When choosing our words, the context in which words are used matters. Even when spoken in jest, a word with a lower frequency will produce that same frequency in the person receiving it and also in water. The water in our body

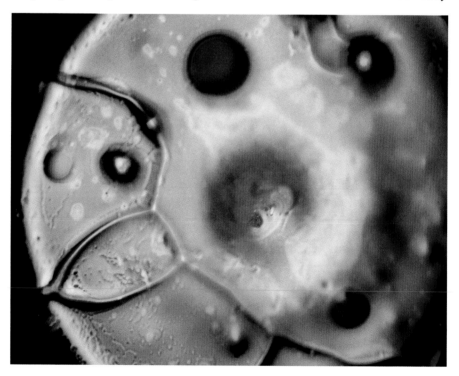

Figure 40. Water shown the word 'dirty'

does not recognize the difference between real or imagined – it just responds to the intrinsic vibration of those words. Let us consider the word 'dirty'. When speaking to a child who comes in from playing outside in the garden, we might say "Oh, you're so dirty", whereas it may be more harmonious to say "Oh look, you have dirt on you". The difference is slight but the change in vibration is significant.

Figure 41. Water shown the word 'cleanliness'

The first sentence "Oh, you're so dirty" states that the child *is* 'dirty', whereas in the second "Oh look, you have dirt on you" states that dirt is on them but they themselves are not dirty. Even though we may not mean to say they are dirty, the vibration of 'dirty' is transmitted through our words and the child can take on a misdirected vibration.

Another example illustrating the power of words is the rice experiment. The following experiment was conducted by Japanese schoolchildren. Ordinary steamed rice was sealed into two glass jars. On one jar the label 'thank you' was placed on one bottle. Every day the schoolchildren said 'thank you' to the jar. On another jar, the label 'you fool' was placed, and every day the schoolchildren said 'you fool' to this bottle (see figure 42).

After three weeks the results were amazing. The rice jar with the 'thank you' label on it smelled rich and mellow like malted rice, looking golden in color, whereas the jar with 'you fool' on it turned black in color and smelled very bad. Because this experiment was very easy to try, many families in Japan and later worldwide tried the experiment with many different variations, and the results

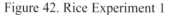

Figure 42. Rice Experiment 1   Figure 43. Rice Experiment 2

were very much the same.

Some months later the IHM Institute received two reports on the results of a new rice experiment. This was conducted by two different families at about the same time. Both families added one more bottle without putting any words on it, in addition to the bottles with 'thank you' and 'you fool' (see figure 43).

The two families had the same results as before, with the rice with the 'thank you' label producing the best results, and the rice with the label 'you fool' becoming rancid. However, what was most startling was the rice which was ignored. The bottle with no words produced the worst result, going rancid faster than the rice labeled 'you fool'. The experimenters jointly concluded that the bottle without any words was the worst *because* it was ignored.

We might apply the same idea to children. A child seeks attention from its parents. If it can't receive positive attention, this may lead to naughty behavior in order to create at least some attention, albeit negative. Being completely ignored is the worst kind of mistreatment, whether it applies to rice, children or anything else.

The rice experiments further illustrate that words have an intrinsic vibration and can have either a positive or negative effect depending upon that vibration.

Another example is the words 'I love you' and 'I hate you'. When you say "I love you" to someone, it creates a feeling of love. By focusing on this feeling of love you might notice changes in your body – changes in your breathing or a sense of calm or warmth. If you become aware of your body it will indicate to you the vibration that comes from the words 'I love you'. Similarly, saying 'I hate you' doesn't have the same feeling when you become aware of your body. You may experience a sinking feeling, or your body might become tight and stressed, and there may be a sense of tension.

One could say that there are really only two emotions, associated with feeling good or feeling bad. We associate all kinds of emotions with good feelings, such as joy, happiness, inspiration and gratitude. We have many emotions associated with bad feelings, such as sorrow, grief, anguish, depression, envy and jealousy. The greater the feelings associated with the emotion the greater the effect.

There is a difference in saying 'I love you' without any feeling behind the words. An empty 'I love you' has a different vibration to one which is said with every fiber of your being. A heart which is fully aligned to love and expressing this emotion fully will have a dramatic increase in the *hado* of love. When we say, 'I hate this' or 'we hated that' in a matter of fact way, without much feeling, it is not the same as delivering these words with a strong feeling of rage and hatred. The *hado* of words spoken with full intention are much stronger in their effect.

The secret is to focus on what you want. The more we focus on emotions on the positive side, the more we will create a vibration of positive emotion in our lives. You cannot be happy if you are constantly speaking words which continually operate from emotions toward the negative side.

Positive emotions are more powerful because of their ability to increase infinitely. Think of a darkened room. As soon as you light a candle, the darkness is instantly dispelled, even though the darkness is big and the light is small. The more we focus on the positive the more powerful it becomes. Negative emotions on the other hand cannot increase infinitely without self-destructing. This is why some people believe there cannot be an absolute principle of evil. If something is completely evil, it will inevitably self-destruct. There are of course many examples where people operate out of a state of ignorance, exhibiting all kinds of disturbing emotions, but it is not uncommon for even the most evil person to exhibit kindness, even if it is just for a pet. It is interesting to note that the word 'evil' is the word 'live', written in reverse. When we live we are in accord with the law of the universe, we expand and grow. To operate from an emotion of evil is to do the very opposite, to contract.

Just as there is a difference between emotions of love and gratitude from a lover or a friend, so there is a difference in love and gratitude for all humanity. I refer here to a love which is unconditional, a love that extends beyond notions of good and bad, that extends infinitely to all things. This has been expressed by His Holiness the Dalai Lama as the 'compassionate heart', a heart which affords compassion to all beings, not just the ones we hold dear. Love and gratitude hold the key to cultivating a compassionate heart. The more we can cultivate the emotion of love and gratitude and extend it to ourselves and others, the more we will become this vibration and attract similar people and circumstances to mirror this state of being.

Words and their meaning

But what of our relationship to words, and how we interpret their meaning? For some the word 'red' can conjure all kinds of emotions. We might associate red with danger, passion, rage or the devil but, in another culture, the color red may have different associations. In China, red is associated with marriage. A Native American might see red as a symbol for the sun. In some respects, a word has an associated feeling for individuals because it is linked to a belief system, a symbol or memory which is culturally related.

Our relationship to words can have a great deal to do with our personal relationships. The word 'God' can mean many things to many people. Mention the word God to a Christian and it will engender an emotion of prayer and devotion. To a Hindu, they might ask 'which one?'. To a Buddhist, they might think its better not to get involved with gods and instead rely on developing one's mind. An atheist might say 'there is no God' and a narcissist might think 'I am God'. One word can mean so much to so many people. If you don't like the word 'God', simply add an 'o' and you'll get the word 'good'. This translates well in any language and is certainly far less complicated.

The power of your name

Names are another example where words have power. When we call a person by their name, we invoke their essence. A person's name represents their spirit or identity, just in the same way a photo of a person holds their intrinsic vibration. If you ever want to try an experiment to prove this to someone, ask a person to write on a piece of paper the name of the person they love and respect the most. It could be a loved one or their beloved pet. Next, ask the person to place the piece of paper with the name on it on the floor. Then tell the person to stomp their feet on the paper with the name and watch their reaction.

I recently conducted this exercise at one of our *hado* seminars with a group of forty participants. It was not at all surprising to me that all forty participants hesitated. But why did they hesitate? It was only a piece of paper with some writing on it. A bunch of letters making up a name… or was there something more? The reason why people hesitated is that, on an intuitive level, they knew the power of words and that a name is intimately connected to the *hado* of that person.

The use of a name to represent another, as a proxy instead of their presence, has been used for centuries in remote healing. To use a person's name is a powerful way to make a connection with them energetically. Healers use a person's name to make a connection, as it becomes a focal point and a way to hone in on the person's energy-body, to allow healing at a distance.

The same is true with our signature. A signature is usually a stylized version of someone's name written on documents as a proof of identity, like a seal. Historically, the use of a signature has existed since the development of print. The Sumerians, who are credited with the invention of writing for business purposes, used seals to authenticate their writings. They applied signatures to their clay writing tablets using rollers. Later, in the Roman Empire, the use of handwritten signatures to authenticate documents began around AD 439, during the rule of Valentinian III. The 'subscripto' was a small handwritten sentence at the end of a document, saying that the signer 'subscribed' to the document.

It was not until 1677 in England that signatures were first legally required.

The English Parliament at this time passed 'An Act for Prevention of Frauds and Perjuries'. The 'Statute of Frauds' (as it became known) required 'some note or memorandum in writing' that was 'signed by the parties' for certain types of transactions.

Today, to sign our name is to express our intention and to give our word. It is to place our seal of approval, to confirm our agreements. But a signature is also an expression of our unique vibration in written form. Each person's signa-

Figure 44. Distilled water shown a picture of cherry blossom flowers

Figure 45. Cherry blossom flowers

Figure 46. Distilled water shown an image of a crop circle. The researcher asked the question "Who made this?"

Figure 47. Distilled water exposed to an image of a crop circle

ture is unique and expresses much about the qualities of a person. When we make our mark, we create a vibration which affirms our intention and holds the key to our personal vibration.

The *hado* of the image

'A picture tells a thousand words', as the saying goes, and nothing could be closer to the truth. Like words, images have an intrinsic vibration. When water is exposed to images which have a pleasant appeal, such as images of nature, water reflects this by forming ordered and structured ice crystals. In some cases, ice crystals will form a structure which actually looks like the image exposed to it.

In figure 44 a bottle of distilled water was placed under a picture of cherry blossom flowers and left overnight. The following day the ice crystals reflected the structure of the flowers, forming beautiful flower-like ice crystal formations. The researchers at IHM have also tested several flowers commonly used in flower essence therapy and the results followed this similar tendency. The ice crystals reflected the shape and characteristics of each flower shown to the water.

Another striking example of water reflecting a message is shown in the example of distilled water placed on an image of a crop circle (figure 47). The researcher asked the question 'Who made this?'. The result is amazing and similar ice crystals formed from the same sample (see figure 46). The obvious result is what appears to be space craft. In this case it seems the water responded to the question. What these images share in common is water's ability to mirror their meaning pictorially.

We might ask the question, "Did the water respond to the projection and expectation of the researcher or was the water revealing a meaning beyond the observer?" I will leave this up to you to answer. Nevertheless, if a picture speaks a thousand words, this ice crystal image certainly does.

The *hado* of music

What of water's ability to receive the *hado* of music? Unlike any other medium, music has the power to uplift, inspire and transform. Most of the research that has been undertaken to date has involved water exposed to classical music, which always forms beautiful ice crystals. Classical music is one of Masaru Emoto's favorite genres, though some songs which include positive words, such as John Lennon's *Imagine* (figure 48) also produced beautiful ice crystals.

Heavy metal music on the other hand formed no ice crystals but instead produced distorted and fragmented formations (figure 49). Now for all those loyal heavy metal fans, this may come as bad news, but what needs to be made clear

Imagine there's no Heaven
It's easy if you try
No hell below us
Above us only sky
Imagine all the people
Living for today

Imagine there's no countries
It isn't hard to do
Nothing to kill or die for
And no religion too
Imagine all the people
Living life in peace

You may say that I'm a dreamer
But I'm not the only one
I hope someday you'll join us
And the world will be as one

Imagine no possessions
I wonder if you can
No need for greed or hunger
A brotherhood of man
Imagine all the people
Sharing all the world

You may say that I'm a dreamer
But I'm not the only one
I hope someday you'll join us
And the world will live as one

Figure 48. John Lennon's *Imagine* played to distilled water

is that the heavy metal song used in this experiment had profane lyrics, and perhaps this is what the water was revealing.

Experiments are yet to be conducted to study different kinds of music fully, but a crucial observation is that it is likely that it is not the genre of music so much as its content and 'vibration' which are the vital factors affecting ice crystal formation.

The lyrics of John Lennon's *Imagine* are included here to reflect upon.

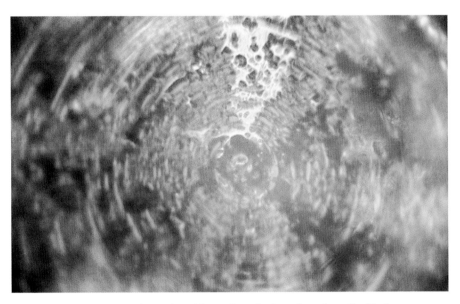

Figure 49. Heavy Metal music with profane lyrics played to distilled water

PART TWO
More about *hado*

CHAPTER 6

THE *HADO* OF PRAYER

The *hado* of Prayer involves the ability to send positive vibrations remotely to bring benefit to a person, a group or a situation. From a quantum perspective, whether a person is next door or in another country, space and time have little bearing on the positive results of prayer. Prayer is therefore not limited by distance or time.

We have all experienced the results of our mind's ability to reach out across space to others. A common example arises when we think about someone and the phone rings and it's the person we were thinking of. Likewise, we might think about a person and soon receive an e-mail from them or bump into them in the street. Some might say this is mere coincidence, but I would venture to say that there are *no* coincidences, and that what we call coincidences is actually only the law of attraction working actively in our lives.

Our mind's ability to span space and even time is operating constantly, expressing infinite possibilities. It is only when we focus our mind into one place that infinite possibilities become finite.

When you ask someone what they mean by the word 'prayer', you may encounter different responses, depending upon the individual's belief system or experience. To a Christian, prayer may create an image of hands folded in supplication, to Buddhist it may be an image of praying for the happiness for all beings, and for a Muslim it may involve gathering together with others to make prayer. Prayer is not just religious. Many secular people would wish an ill person to get well or wish hard to win the lottery. For a lover of football, prayer might mean wishing their team will win, and for a mechanic it might mean praying that an engine will work.

Prayer takes many forms and means many things for many people. In my own experience, it has two main forms. The first is a prayer for asking – for a boon, for healing or for something for us or another person, or for protection or for an illness to abate.

The second kind of prayer is a prayer of thanks. We are acknowledging what we have or have received. Imagine a world that prayed every day with gratitude and thanks. Sometimes, when there is a disaster or humanitarian crisis, large numbers of people pray for the victims' wellbeing, even following it up with donations too.

Prayer need not be a formal event. It can be as simple as seeing an elderly woman on the bus and thinking 'I hope she makes it', or the joy that comes from seeing that she did make it. Prayer is a sincere heart wishing for another being to be happy, or for things to turn out well, and it might be that spontaneous prayers are the most powerful. For some people prayer is a last resort: when faced with danger or pain, or when death is close at hand, a prayer is often offered, even by the most skeptical of people.

I was brought up a Christian and, as a good Christian, I went to church, prayed for my family or for my life, but my prayers were always asking God for something. I always felt that God must have been really busy attending to the prayers of millions of Christians, and this was probably the reason he had not gotten back to me. Yet despite my continued waiting for the results, I nevertheless felt a certain grace that came from prayer. Whether or not my prayers were answered, didn't matter a great deal. In retrospect the very act of praying brought with it comfort and grace. Later I came to know that there was a different kind of prayer – a prayer of appreciation and an acknowledgement of the things I did have. This had a different feeling. It felt unencumbered, expansive and warmed-up.

I see prayer as a desire from the depth of our being to cultivate happiness, for ourselves or for others. This search for happiness can be approached in an outward sense or cultivated inwardly. Whichever approach is used, the very act of prayer generates something. While results may not manifest in the world in the way we might imagine, the doing of prayer is what matters.

For many, the very thought of prayer brings up some resistance. One might associate it with religious dogma or some kind of 'deal-making' with a particular God. We might form this idea due to a generally misunderstood relationship with God or consciousness. We need really to drop our associations with prayer and our concerns about what or whom we pray to, and approach prayer with a sense of openness. In Chapter Eight I share an alternative way of '*hado* prayer' which might help.

The *Hado* of intention

I wish to tell you of a personal experience of *hado* in action. In April 2006 I took a group of my Reiki students on a tour to the historical places of interest in the lineage of Reiki healing. During our visit we had the unique opportunity to visit the IHM research center in Tokyo, where our practitioners participated in a water blessing experiment to see how Reiki affects the tap water of Tokyo.

Knowing that Reiki has positive effects upon water, we wanted to see if we could collectively have an effect on the water. We arrived at IHM and were warmly welcomed by IHM's president Mr Hazaka. Armed only with our 'Reiki hands' we were given the option to conduct the experiment using distilled water (favored for higher results) or to take the challenge to see if Reiki could recover Tokyo tap water, which produces no ice crystals when tested.

In all the IHM experiments conducted over the years, Tokyo tap water has never formed ice crystals due to the heavy chlorine content of the water (see figure 52). Obtaining an ice crystal from Tokyo tap water using only Reiki energy would be a world first. Not wanting to let a challenge like that slip by, we chose

Figure 50. Reiki practitioners with their hands held in 'Gassho' (prayer gesture) prior to directing Reiki to Tokyo tap water

the tap water over the distilled water.

To conduct the experiment we formed a circle and directed Reiki healing without touching the water sample. After only five minutes of directing Reiki energy we all felt more peaceful and were excited to see if our experiment bore good results. One week later, after our return to Australia, we received some exciting news. Our experiment was a great success. After directing Reiki to Tokyo tap water, the water was transformed at the molecular level. Several samples revealed ice crystal formations and the crystals seemed to clearly illustrate the value of the brief but powerful water blessing.

Figure 51. Reiki Practitioners directing Reiki to Tokyo tap water

The ice crystal in figure 53 shows a seven-sided formation. It is interesting to note that seven Reiki practitioners participated in the water blessing. Another ice crystal from the same sample produced an interesting formation too (see figure 12).

A simple method of blessing water is explained in detail in Chapter Eight. By following the

Figure 52. Tokyo tap water sample before Reiki experiment

procedure for blessing water you will be pleasantly surprised by the difference you can make. So much so, that you can actually taste the difference in the water, before and after.

Figure 53. An ice crystal sample of Tokyo tap water after Reiki was directed to it by seven Reiki Practitioners

CHAPTER 7

THE POWER OF *HADO*

So far we have explored a number of water's amazing qualities and how we can imprint our conscious intention upon it. But what drives this ability and what is *hado*?

In order to understand these principles we first need to understand the meaning of *hado*, the Japanese word for frequency or wave. Its meaning extends to the subtle energy that exists in the universe. Everything has a *hado*. In Japan the name is commonly used in numerous settings. When someone enters a room they might comment on the *hado* of the space, saying "This place has a nice vibe." We can all probably relate to this when we visit a new place for the first time. What we are really relating to is the *hado* of the environment. We might also encounter a new person and, if we feel good about them, we resonate with them, and we are relating to their *hado* in a positive way because it resonates well with our vibration.

Another way to describe *hado* would be 'The Force' as described in *Star Wars* – and, yes, there is a light and dark side. When someone is operating with their disturbed emotions, they are not recognizing the true nature of how things are, and they can even make matters worse than they are. Positive *hado* on the other hand represents a state of mind which sees more clearly and knows how things are. Positive *hado* operates in tune with the higher principles of subtle energy.

When you meet a person and instantly take a dislike to them, you could say that you are not resonating with them or that your *hado* does not fit with theirs. Another person might meet the very same person and instantly 'hit it off'. Is the person in question exhibiting two different kinds of *hado*, or is the other person resonating with a similar vibration to them? The latter is possibly true, but what is also true is our ability to adjust our *Hado* according to any given situation.

Sympathetic resonance

We can illustrate *hado* in terms of 'sympathetic resonance'. Sympathetic resonance occurs when one resonating vibration affects another and causes it to resonate in harmony. Take two guitars tuned to the same key. Pluck the string of one guitar and the other guitar will begin to vibrate with the same note. This resonance is based on the universal law of attraction – like attracts like. This law of attraction is called *entrainment*. This phenomenon was first recognized by Christian Huygens in the seventeenth century.

Entrainment is a process whereby one frequency or vibration aligns with or matches another. Huygens was an inventor of pendulum clocks and owned a vast collection of them. One day he noticed that all of the pendulums were swinging in unison, which puzzled him as he had not originally set them this way. So he went about setting the pendulums to different rhythms to see if they would align once again. Sure enough, within a few days all of the pendulums began to swing in perfect unison. He found that they aligned to the pendulum with the strongest rhythm.

The same is true for human beings. Take a group of people and the person with the strongest *hado* will emerge as the group leader. One could call this magnetism or charisma. A magnetic person will have a greater capacity to attract others to their way of thinking or will be able to lead a group of people to their particular way of thinking.

A tuning fork also acts in a similar way. Take three tuning forks (see figure 54). Two tuning forks are set at 440Hz and the third is set at 442Hz. The range of hearing for the average person is between 20 to 20,000Hz and one hertz is equal to one vibration per second. When hitting one of the 440Hz tuning forks with a rubber hammer, the second 440 Hz tuning fork will also resonate, but the one tuning fork set at 442 Hz will make no sound at all. Although the 442Hz tuning fork sounds the same as 440Hz to the human ear it nonetheless makes no vibration as the frequency is not compatible. This is because, when two things have the same resonance, they vibrate together, whereas when there is dissonance, there can not be the same resonance occurring, due to a lack of compatibility. We know this to be true with other frequencies. For example, the human ear cannot hear the high frequency of a dog whistle, though your four-legged friend will begin to howl when hearing one.

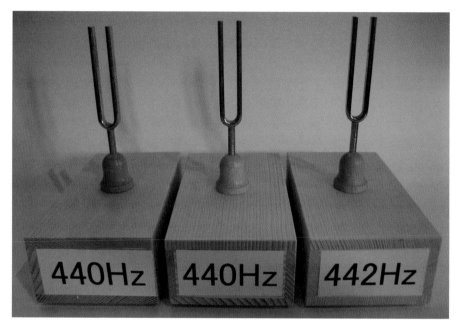

Figure 54. Tuning Forks. By striking the middle tuning fork only, the left tuning fork (440Hz), tuned to the same frequency, resonates while the 442 Hz on the right, although sounding the same, does not resonate

Sympathetic resonance is in operation all the time. How often have we met a person and resonated with them? We use the language, "I really resonate with what you are saying," or "We are on the same wavelength." On the level of *hado* this is precisely what is happening. Our vibration matches and we instantly 'hit it off'.

You may also have noticed what happens to perfectly normal adults when they play with small children or talk to babies. Their voices often become higher. The key reason for this is that they are resonating with the babies' frequency, and their voice becomes higher to match the *hado* of the infant.

This relationship of resonance is due to everything having an intrinsic vibration. At the subatomic level this intrinsic vibration interacts with other subatomic particles. This interaction is happening all the time. For the most part we don't notice it. More than anything we sense it in the form of our daily interactions where we feel 'in tune' or 'out of tune' with others. This is an experience of resonance.

The *hado* of anger

We all experience ups and downs in life. We can therefore say we have good *hado* days and bad *hado* days. Have you ever got up from the wrong side of the bed in the morning and experienced a day where everything seems to go wrong? When a day like this happens we see the world through dark colored glasses. Everything and everyone is the cause of our unhappy situation. Perhaps the toast burned in the morning and we ran out of coffee. Then the bus driver was in a grumpy mood, the boss was upset with you and for some reason your computer crashed just prior to backing up your data. What could it all mean? Is it that the world is conspiring against you? The answer is in how we are operating from our inner perspective. When we are operating with negative *hado* the outer environment mirrors this back to us. Because our *hado* is negative, we attract and resonate with people with a similar negative vibration matching our mindset.

When we are operating with negative *hado*, we draw to us circumstances which will support our negative vibration. When we are angry, nothing flows. Some modern-day psychologists have advocated expressing our anger – by voicing our anger we will liberate it – but in fact what happens is that the pattern of anger is reinforced.

Getting angry does not benefit anyone, least of all yourself. When we get angry we produce harmful chemicals in our bodies, our face becomes red and ugly. Anger is like a thief who has stolen our beauty. Have you ever seen an angry person look beautiful? When anger takes hold, we can harm both ourselves and others, either verbally or physically. An outburst of anger also destroys many positive impressions which have been built up in our store consciousness. When we get angry, use harsh words or generate negative impressions, the water in our body becomes distorted and ugly.

So what is the remedy? For those of us with a short fuse we can implement some simple remedies. The first is to remove yourself from the situation. You might be having an argument with your spouse and you can feel anger rising. You know you are about to get into a heated argument and it could escalate further. The remedy is to stop what you are doing and remove yourself from the situation. You might say, "I feel I am getting angry, so I am going to take a break and will continue this once I've cooled down."

I know of a friend who had an anger problem, particularly on the telephone. Whenever he felt he was getting hot under the collar, he simply said, "Hang on, I'll call you back in fifteen minutes." He'd get up, walk around the block and focus on some deep calming breaths. By the time he got back, he felt calmer and had obtained some distance from the situation. With some space from the situation he could address the issue with greater ease. Distance in this case is one way to overcome anger.

Another remedy is to look at anger like a thief who has come to your house to steal your belongings. The trick is to let the thief come to an empty house. This means not to allow anger to be given a voice. When we feel anger arising, we give it nothing. We simply let it arise and, provided we give it no attention, it will subside because we are not fueling it. We starve the emotion until it gives up. This may not be so easy in the heat of the moment but with practice and awareness you will be more able to operate in this way.

At this level, anger is like a thief who comes to your house and the door is left open. You leave the door open so anger can walk in, but to anger's surprise the house is empty. Anger will look around, trying to find something to steal but, if we remain vigilant and do nothing to aid anger's hold, it will simply leave empty-handed.

When anger is on its way out, this is when you can put anger's residual energy to work. Physical activity is useful when anger has subsided. You can use the energy which has arisen from the anger. This is like getting the thief to do the dishes on the way out. But be careful that you are over the crest of the wave of anger before you put anger to work, otherwise you might end up breaking the dishes, cutting your hand and getting wet.

The emotion of anger not only applies to reactions to life's challenging situations. It also applies to anything we have a mild aversion to. When we come to know what triggers our anger we can understand how to defuse it. As a result, it will no longer have the hold it once had. The best antidote to anger is to feed it love and gratitude. Instead of a feast of aggression and aversion, a diet of love and gratitude makes anger weak. It will not grow but lose weight. With enough love and gratitude in your daily diet, anger will have no chance to steal your beauty.

Anger, like other disturbing emotions, affects the *hado* in our body. We might imagine what kind of ice crystals we could create from water in our body with an increase of positive emotions. The water in our body is super-sensitive to thoughts, feelings and emotions, so in cultivating love and gratitude we will give rise to positive *hado* and the *hado* of happiness in our daily lives. The good news is that we can change our *hado* in any given moment. We have a choice in the way we view reality.

The *hado* of happiness

The *hado* of happiness has an ability to grow, provided we nurture it. We need to care for it like a seedling which has been freshly planted in the garden of consciousness. The *hado* of happiness does not arise from fleeting moments of relative happiness that come from events and fortunes around us, such as the happiness of an encounter with a lover, or arising from a compliment or the acquisition of more 'stuff'. This is a happiness that is slowly cultivated from the inside which is not dependant upon external circumstances to make it grow and stay.

When we look at happiness, there are two kinds. The first is the happiness which comes from external influences, such as a new job promotion, a new relationship, a new car or the acquisition of material things. These are all sources which are constantly changing and, because of their impermanent nature, they cannot satisfy us in a lasting way, and sooner or later they also leave us. We might buy the latest BMW and enjoy initial feelings of happiness, but for how long? After some time, the happiness associated with the car will begin to fade. It might receive a scratch or dent or something might break. Suddenly the focus will change, turning to car loan repayments, the sinking value of the car or the next model soon to come out. The problem with this kind of happiness is its impermanent nature. The happiness comes and goes when circumstances or our feelings about them change.

I am not suggesting that if we do without material things, pack up our gear, sell them and go and live in a cave, we will be happier. A car can be useful and so can a house and relationship. It is fine to have things, but it is important not to see them solely as a source of happiness and become attached to them. If we see material objects as sources of happiness we will surely be disappointed. So what is the alternative? The answer lies in finding happiness within ourselves. This brings us to the second kind of happiness, the happiness that comes from within.

One of the best ways to cultivate the *hado* of happiness is to change our point of view. In the beginning a 'fake it till you make it' principle may predominate until the *hado* of happiness becomes a more normal experience in our minds. In the beginning we may see the world as a glass half empty. But the more we cultivate the *hado* of happiness, the more we will be able to generate a view of the glass being half full.

One of the most effective ways to generate this is to think about the welfare of others. When we are self-absorbed it is hard to see the joy in our world and the joy in others. By cultivating sympathetic joy, we can grow the *hado* of happiness in ourselves.

The happiness which is most reliable is the happiness from within. This may seem obvious but, for most people, this is the last place they look. How do we cultivate an experience of inner happiness? We need to cultivate our positive *hado* and purify our negative *hado*.

A prime cause of problems is our strong attachment to external circumstances and holding on to fixed ideas based on past experiences. When we have a difficult experience we can either let it become a part of our reality or look at it as something transitory. Whilst on holiday with a friend of mine I suggested that we go out one night for dinner. He said this would be fine as long as we didn't eat in a Thai restaurant. I asked why and he recalled a time five years before when we got sick from eating Thai food in a restaurant in his old home town. From this one-off experience he had decided that all Thai food makes you sick. The restaurant had probably had a bad run that day. The fact was, five years had passed and it wasn't even the same restaurant, nor was it the same town, yet the conditioned experience remained.

Many of us operate our lives in this way. We could have repeating good meals at a restaurant and, the one time we have a difficult experience, we forget all of the prior positive experiences. All we remember is the negative experience, which we hold on to and can live out for the rest of our days. When we encounter a negative experience we should aim to remedy the situation as soon as possible, to prevent a pattern from stabilizing in the mind. My friend should have decided that, next time he ate out, it should again be Thai food, just to ensure that a pattern did not lodge in his mind-stream. Get back on that horse, the moment you are thrown, rather than deciding that you are beaten because of one experience.

The longer we leave negative experiences unresolved, the greater the imprint becomes. A new pattern of reality is created and stored. Each time we think of the negative situation, we reinforce a belief which, in most cases, has no real basis. We need to recognize that everything is constantly changing. This frees us from a perpetual cycle of good and bad, positive and negative. We can instead view reality as a life-stream full of endless potential and possibilities.

Because we are endlessly fascinated by objects in the mirror, we fail to recognize the mirror itself. We get caught up in dramas, rather than recognizing they are empty in nature. By using the word empty, does not mean a black hole: it represents the spaciousness that comes from recognizing that, whatever is experienced, the experience and the act of experiencing are part of the same totality. There is no separation between subject, object and action.

How others affect our vibration

Have you ever met someone who you would describe as a person with low vibration? Just spending five minutes with them seems like an eternity and, within a short time, your mood becomes diminished just by being in their presence. This is where negative *hado* rubs off. It is not that we have decided that we will take on their vibration – it just happens. We may even deeply care for that person but, by spending time with them, their imbalanced energy field mixes with ours and our *hado* is diminished.

On the flip side, you have probably also encountered someone who is always optimistic and a good influence. No matter what happens to them, they always see the positive in everything. Even when the chips are stacked against them, they maintain a cheerful disposition. The woes of the world just don't stick. By spending just five minutes with them, the vibration of their happiness becomes infectious. We do not consciously make a decision that, by spending time with them we will 'get happy', but the higher vibration of that person's energy field mixes with ours and we cannot help but feel happy.

Though some may find this kind of happy behavior unusual, the optimistic person has much to teach us. The secret is that, whether we 'fake it till we make it' or genuinely feel positive, our body and mind do not know the difference. The more we focus on what is positive, the more we attract more of the same, and the more we re-wire and re-program our brains to match our thoughts. We therefore have a choice to spend time with people and in circumstances that will influence us with positive or negative *hado*.

The same is true on the telephone. You can be on a call to someone and, if they are feeling down or sad, it is hard not to get caught up in their problems. *Hado* is not bound by time or space. Whether you are talking to a person in front of you or in another country, it makes no difference to the energy of *hado*. It is always experienced directly. It is all too easy to get caught up in negative *hado* conversations. Gossip and talking about other people's problems on the telephone are hazardous and can feed negative *hado* for all parties involved. Negativity can spread quickly and, even though you are not in a person's presence, you may as well be.

The same is true for text-messaging or e-mail. Try to keep your emails positive and be vigilant of the words you use. All words have *hado* and spirit. The words we use can communicate harmony and love or division and harm. If we wish to develop positive *hado* and better ourselves and the world around us, we need to take charge of the words we use.

Hado and correct speech

When we gossip about others, we create division. Bad news travels fast and, sooner or later, gossip makes the round and the person who is the object of such conversations gets hurt. If you are around others who love to gossip, simply take a stand and suggest that it would be better if they speak to the person concerned, face to face. Another option is to change the subject to something more positive, or remove yourself from the situation. If you can't say something good about someone, better to say nothing at all. We create only disharmony by focusing on problems. What we focus upon, we amplify.

You may protest, saying that gossip is harmless. Although tittle-tattle is not as harmful as gossip where we are actively creating or spreading rumors, it nevertheless creates a vibration of discord. Each of us must make a personal choice concerning speech which is divisive or contributes to negative *hado*.

There are times when we might come across really tough customers and find it hard to find good qualities them. The person in question may be an expert in creating problems. This is where compassion comes in. Think of the other person for a minute. They have to spend all day and night living with themselves. Looking at it this way, we see the suffering they cause themselves. Thinking this way, it is hard not to generate compassion.

We might also consider the words we use on a daily level to reinforce our belief-systems. As we speak, so we become. Have you ever thought about your negative speech? For many, these negative reinforcements are so heavily ingrained, they come naturally.

Do some of these ring any bells? "I'm sick and tired of being late." "So-and-so is a pain in the neck." "I'm starving!" "I'm dying for some coffee." "I'd kill for some pizza." "My back is killing me!" "You're always…" (insert problem). "I feel like crap" (or your noun of choice). "Your hands are filthy!" "I hate…" (name the thing, situation or person). "You're making me feel…" (insert problem). "You're driving me insane!"

How many sayings like these do we unconsciously use each day? This is 'hazardous speech'. Hazardous speech steals positive *hado*. As we have seen through the images of ice crystals exposed to negative words, negative reinforcements create distorted formations, and if our thoughts can do this to water, imagine what our thoughts are doing to us.

To take this a step further, what are our thoughts doing to others and to our fragile world? Do we actually help our politicians behave better by directing negative *hado* their way? Do we help our children behave better by constantly reinforcing our judgments about how bad their behavior is? Do we grow as human beings by constantly telling ourselves how we have failed, or by telling others what is wrong with us? Maybe we need to change. Maybe we need to ask ourselves what is right with ourselves and acknowledge what is worth celebrating. It is about waking up to self-awareness. If anything, water is revealing this message.

The *hado* of self-love

More often than not, we are our own worst judge and jury. Many people are very critical about their looks or their level of performance. How often do we look in the mirror first thing in the morning and say "Hello, beautiful!"? Many people begin the day by observing their flaws. It can be a real challenge to start your day well. It is for this reason that we need to consciously cultivate the positive *hado* of self-love. Self-love is not thinking how great we are, but celebrating our 'greatness'. To love ourselves is a wonderful thing. Just look how beautiful water becomes when shown the words 'self-love' in figure 55. If loving ourselves can create water like this, you might re-think how you look at yourself in the mirror each day.

Figure 55. Water shown the words 'self-love' (in Japanese, *Jikoai*)

The *hado* of truth

One of the best ways to remedy some of the harm we create through our speech is to speak truth. When we tell untruths or lies, we create a misalignment and make our lives more complicated. When we lie we block our freedom because telling lies binds us to mistruth. People mostly tell untruths to give themselves an advantage – they are almost always for self-benefit. We also lie so that we can be important, or believe we are more or better than we are. As a result we feel superior living under an illusion that we have gained something extra. What actually happens is that we betray our true nature and create a separation between ourselves and others.

When you tell an untruth, within a short period of time you will need to tell another to back up the previous one, then another to back up the second, and then another and another. Before long you are like a person juggling several balls in the air all at once. The more lies you tell, the harder it becomes to keep all of the lies actively in the air at one time. It is only a matter of time before the untruths come crashing down. Keeping lies active requires considerable effort and you can never truly relax, as you have to focus so much energy preserving them.

So how to we prevent ourselves from lying? There are three ways. The first is to catch yourself when you are in the middle of an untruth and stop. Say something like, "I'm sorry, that wasn't true, and what I meant to say was…" The second is to catch yourself when the lie is forming in your head. If you are fast enough you'll notice that you are preparing an untruth and are about to unleash it. Again, stop before you speak and speak truth instead. The third way is to notice the energy that comes just prior to formulating a lie. Allow the energy of mistruth to rise, and give it nothing. It will fall and dissolve back into awareness. When you accept how things are and honor your path and others' paths, the need to lie disappears. You don't create so much trouble and you honor your development without getting in the way of yourself or others.

Of course there are times when telling a lie can be good, especially when it is to benefit another. There is a story of an old man sitting under a tree. Suddenly, from out of nowhere, a man comes running by shouting, "Please help me! Some men are chasing me and will kill me, so if I hide in the tree above you, will you say I am not here?" The old man under the tree says yes, and the man climbs up to hide in the foliage. Soon the other men pass by. They see the old man at the base of the tree and ask, "Did you see a man running by here a few minutes ago?" The old man says nothing but points in the direction down the track. The men thank him and run off continuing their search.

In this story, is it a good or a bad lie to protect the man hiding in the tree? Perhaps the man hiding in the tree was a bandit, a thief or a murderer, or perhaps he was an innocent person seeking refuge from unfortunate events. Nevertheless it is not up to the old man under the tree to pass judgment but to preserve a life.

There is another story of a thief who comes into the house of a monk to steal his humble belongings. The thief sees the monk meditating. To his surprise the monk says, "Please take anything you like. My belongings are for everyone. All I ask is that you say thank you when you are leaving." The thief is very surprised by the monk's words, but he sees the opportunity given to him and takes all of the monk's possessions. As the thief is leaving the monk reminds him to say thank you. The thief laughs but says "Thank you" as he leaves, somewhat puzzled.

Sometime later there is a knock at the door. The police have caught the thief and returned with the monk's possessions. The police say, "We caught this man stealing your things and he will now be severely prosecuted." In the thief's defense, the monk says, "Oh no, there has been a misunderstanding. I gave all these items to him, and he even said thank you." The police, after some thought, agreed and set the thief free. After the police left, the thief questioned the monk about the reason for his extraordinary display of kindness. The monk said that, in order to prevent the thief from accumulating further unfortunate karma, he created a way to prevent this by freely giving his possessions.

He taught the thief to take only that which is freely given. Upon hearing this teaching, the thief was moved. Something stirred inside him and he knew that, from that point on, he needed to live a wholesome life. He decided then and there to become a disciple of the monk and steadfastly studied meditation. In time he achieved many positive accomplishments and later became a teacher of meditation.

As this story illustrates, there are times when we may lie to benefit another, but a lie for selfish reasons never benefits anyone. We should do our best to be truthful in all our activities. When we speak truth, we radiate truth in all directions, we shine a light for all to see our inner beauty and we create a truthful world. Much like the beautiful ice crystal of water shown the word 'truth' in figure 56, the truth will set you free.

The *hado* of sound and vision

What kind of visual and auditory diet are you on? We all know that, if we feed ourselves fast food and overindulge in drugs or alcohol, we will be on a gradual path of self-destruction. But what of the food we feed our eyes and ears? Through Masaru Emoto's experiments, it has been determined that wholesome television shows and films which inspire and uplift the heart generate beautiful ice crystals and, similarly, unwholesome programs, violent films and similar create distorted ice crystals. It is not such a great leap to recognize that what we watch and listen to will affect our body and mind.

It is therefore important to be mindful what we choose to take in, and how much we choose to watch television or watch films. Films with graphic violence and coarse language will diminish our positive *hado*. Although intellectually you

Figure 56. Distilled water shown the word Truth

know it's just a movie, your brain does not really recognize the difference. You can be watching a scary movie and, at a climatic scene, you jump in your chair, your heart is racing and your body is responding as if it were real. Body and mind are responding, and we generate a vibration to match our external input. We have all had the experience of being swept away by a movie. Like a discerning person, I suggest you be aware of what you see and how certain films and programs affect you.

The same is true of video games. Although it is 'make-believe', when you are fighting aliens or shooting enemies, the *hado* in your body is being affected. There are of course many games which do not have a violent nature, so it is better to choose games with a lighter subject, especially for children.

When it comes to the radio, a great deal of talkback radio is negative in its direction. Stations with lots of advertising should also be avoided. We are constantly being bombarded with messages and most do not assist the growth of *hado*.

The news is another powerful tool to spread fear. The global 'war on terror' can't be assisting generation of the *hado* of peace. We won't generate peace if we focus on war. What we focus upon is what we create. If we keep feeding our mind with fear, this is what we will become, and we generate a vibration to match our reality.

I personally like to keep up to date with world events and I do watch television briefly, as I feel it is responsible to know what is going on around the world. But I choose to limit which channels I watch and for how long. I avoid commercial stations from the big networks, so that I do not have to subject myself to relentless advertising. If you must watch commercial television, try pressing the 'mute' button when advertising is on or, better still, get out of your chair and visit nature, or do something creative. There is more to life than what is on the 'boob-tube'.

I am not suggesting that you can't enjoy a good action movie, thriller or drama. It just depends on the content and how it affects you on an energetic level. Unless you are prepared never to read a newspaper, own a TV or listen to the radio, you'll never completely avoid being exposed to negative information. We can make a choice, however, to navigate through this landscape with awareness. Make choices which support your lifestyle and wellbeing. Just as eating fast food for three meals a day is not good for you, so also three hours of television will more than likely make your mind overweight and deplete your *hado*.

The *hado* of the Internet

The internet offers a virtual world where we can view just about everything from the weird to the wonderful. It is perhaps the best vehicle for free speech and is widely available to everyone. But just as words direct *hado* into our lives and can reaffirm our beliefs, for better or for worse, so it is when we use the Internet. We can choose where we go and what we feed into our minds.

When water was shown the word for the Internet it produced the water crystal in figure 57. It is as if water is showing the ability to reproduce information with a double ice crystal, one growing out of the other. For all the negative *hado* which resides in cyberspace, we may conclude that there is more positive *hado* than there is negative, as the ice crystal formed a hexagonal structure with beautiful branches. This demonstrates the Internet's ability to share and to educate. What we choose to learn and expose ourselves to is a choice we all make each time we sit in front of the computer.

Figure 57. Water shown the words 'the Internet'

The *hado* of illness

When someone experiences an illness their *hado* is out of alignment. Every illness has a specific vibration and an associated disturbing emotion attributed to it. Worry, for example, is one of the primary causes of illness. In Table One are several examples demonstrating where certain emotions contribute to disease, where these imbalances commonly translate in the body, and the corresponding canceling emotion.

Of course this is just an overview, as there are many contributing factors which cause illnesses and imbalances. Perhaps the best way to look at illness is through our energy-body. All illness manifests due to a maladjustment in our energy system. These maladjustments are caused by certain factors, which include:

- Our words, thoughts, and actions
- Cause and effect
- Our genetic tendencies
- The way we either nurture or harm our bodies
- Our energetic and physical environment
- Our emotions, values and beliefs.

Our thoughts and actions sow the seeds for our future. Our previous thoughts and actions influence our present state of health. As we think, so we become. If we think, say or carry out things which are harmful, we sow future difficulties.

This brings us to cause and effect. The things we have done, said and thought sowed the seeds for our present circumstances. If we experience illness and difficulty, it is due to our previous unskillful actions. We have an opportunity to learn patience and to choose not to add to future misfortune by reacting negatively in such moments.

The third point is our genetic proclivity or tendency. Our parents' gene pool determines what type of body and tendencies we have and, while our lives are not directly determined by these, we nevertheless need to recognize propensities we have acquired from them.

The fourth point includes outer influences, including the types of food and drink we ingest. Certain foods and substances will have a good or harmful effect on our bodily systems. If we choose to harm our bodies through overindulgence, we inevitably cause illness and harm to ourselves.

The fifth point is our environment. This concerns not only our physical exposure to certain chemicals, viruses and germs, but the energetic environments that we choose to live and spend time in. This includes people we live with, friends we have and the kinds of work we do. All these have a direct effect on our health and peace of mind.

The sixth point is related to our emotions, values and beliefs. It is well documented that, with a positive mind, our bodily system positively responds, and when we have negative emotions our body becomes sick and unbalanced. These changes appear to a greater or lesser extent from changes in our emotions. If we are exposed to lower vibrations, this in turn affects our energy body, which in turn creates illness, disharmony and disease.

When we do, think and say things which are not beneficial, this creates a cause. These causes will either manifest in our lives in the present moment, or they will serve as the seeds of future problems. When negative actions ripen, illness and disharmony will be the result. We become a magnet for what we put out.

The good news is we can do much to prevent illness and misfortune. All we need to do is apply a good dose of positive *hado* and we will experience a restoration to a state of balance and harmony.

One of the best ways to deal with obstacles is to give up harmful words, thoughts and actions and replace these with positive words, thoughts and actions. When we begin to appreciate ourselves and others, truly wishing the best, this energy of appreciation becomes a catalyst for good health and balance in our bodies and thus in our minds.

The following chart looks at some of the common negative emotions we experience, their relationship with certain organs and the potential results of expressing these emotions. It also offers positive emotions which can remedy the causes.

HADO OF EMOTION	ORGANS RESONATING WITH EMOTIONS	HADO OF DISEASE	CANCELLING EMOTIONS
Stress	Intestines	Indigestion	Relaxation
Worry	Cervical nerves	Stiff shoulders	Easygoingness
Irritability	Parasympathetic nerves	Insomnia	Calmness
Perplexity	Autonomic nerves	Low-back pain	Good grace
Excess fear	Kidneys	Renal diseases	Peace of mind
Anxiety	Stomach	Dyspepsia	Relief
Anger	Liver	Hepatitis	Compassion
Apathy	Spine	Weakened vitality	Passion
Impatience	Pancreas	Diabetes	Tolerance
Loneliness	Brain's hippocampus	Senile dementia	Pleasure
Sadness	Blood	Leukemia	Joy
Grudge	Skin	Skin ulceration	Gratitude

Table 1. *Hado* relations between emotions and the body parts.
Table courtesy of Masuru Emoto, from his book *The True Power of Water.*

The information in Table One is by no means exclusive or an all-encompassing form of diagnosis, but it illustrates some of the general tendencies arising from engaging in negative emotions. One could say that having negative emotions is like having an expensive friend: if they never have any money, we cannot afford to keep them, since they cost us too much. Though this friend may appear familiar, they can steal your happiness. The more we open ourselves to positive emotions such as love and gratitude, the more we will create health and happiness in our lives.

The *hado* of love and gratitude

When we are out of balance with our emotions we become magnets for negative situations and for people who reflect our negative affirmations. When we operate out of appreciation, we emit positive *hado* and thus attract to ourselves positive situations which reflect our positive affirmation.

The more we generate positive emotions, the better we will feel. Ultimately we become more balanced. The body and mind are intimately connected and we cannot maintain a happy attitude for too long without beneficially affecting the body. Conversely, a well and healthy person who is constantly angry and depressed will eventually cultivate illness or misfortune through continued disturbing emotions.

The heart is also greatly affected by our emotions. Take the emotions of love and gratitude verses those of hate and anger. When someone experiences the emotion of anger, real or imagined, the heart's rhythm becomes disordered and fluctuating. This sets off a number of chain reactions in the body. Blood pressure rises, blood vessels constrict and skin color changes. Have you observed a person 'boiling with anger'? The person will often become red in the face and upper body.

Conversely, when a person generates an emotion of love and gratitude the rhythm of the heart becomes harmonious, steady and exhibits a balanced wave. When we are operating from this positive emotion our immune function is enhanced, our nervous system functions well and our hormonal balance is improved. These changes in heart rhythm were observed by researchers Doc Lew Childre and Howard Martin in their book *The Heart Math Solution.* What their research confirms is that when we are in a state of gratitude and appreciation our entire body, mind and emotions are enhanced. Love and gratitude have the power to heal and transform our body and mind.

The *hado* of cooking

A meal cooked with love tastes better. When we have a good meal, it tastes great as you taste the positive *hado* within it. Whether a chef has taken pride in his cooking or a home-cooked meal has been prepared with love, it is not only the skill of the cook and the quality of the ingredients that matter (though these are important), it is the positive love of the person who prepared it that makes the big difference.

Cooking invariably involves the use of water, whether it is used to wash the vegetables, or water is used to boil the food, water is always present. If a person is preparing food with love and gratitude, with the intention that the food will benefit those who will eat it, the positive *hado* of love will be imprinted into the food.

If we cook while in a bad mood we may well serve ourselves and others a bad meal. If you are in a foul mood, avoid cooking altogether. There is no point in taking out your frustrations on the salad and thereby imbuing the food with negative *hado*. The result will be that you will eat that negativity or, worse, offer it to others. You are effectively ingesting a bad mood. It is better not eat a meal prepared by an angry chef or family member. But if you must, do something to revive the positive *hado* within it. When we honor food and give thanks for it, we increase its vibratory level.

When eating out, in most cases you will not know who prepared your meal, let alone what mood they are in. I always bless my food with *hado* (see chapter 8) to ensure the vibration of the food is rebalanced and enhanced. Of course, if a meal is really bad, a short blessing will not save a meal.

To give a funny example, whilst traveling in Japan, a friend and I had to take an early train to the airport. As we had little time for breakfast, we decided to get a quick take-away. At this early hour there was nothing open, but we really wanted a hot drink to combat the icy cold morning air. So we walked the streets of Tokyo searching in vain for a coffee shop. Finally, with only minutes to spare, we found a dingy coffee shop selling percolated coffee. By then we were in a hurry. The coffee looked really bad but we took it anyway, against our better judgment, in the hope that something miraculous would transform the coffee.

The miracle did not happen. The coffee was severely burnt, the water was overly hot and the powered milk didn't remember its former origins. We decided to give Reiki a try and energized the takeaway cup for ten minutes or so. By then the coffee had cooled a little but the taste had not improved. It goes to show that some things can't be improved.

The difference between meals cooked with love and fast food are enormous. The ice crystal which formed from the words 'mother's cooking' (figure 58) was a perfectly-formed ice crystal. When water was shown the words 'fast food' (figure 59), we see an image which looks a bit like a fast food package.

At the third *Hado* Instructors' School held by Masaru Emoto in Hawaii, I recall that, when the participants saw the ice crystal image for 'fast food' for the first time, many of them laughed. Someone called out, "It looks like a frozen meal for one!" Another person said, "It's like a pizza box!" Everyone had a good laugh, but it is interesting to note that, out of fifty samples tested for water shown the words 'fast food', this was the best ice crystal to be found. All but a few of the samples produced crystals and none had any beautiful structure.

Figure 58. Water shown the words 'mother's cooking'

Figure 59. Water shown the words 'fast food'

When we consider how most fast food is prepared, not a great deal of love and gratitude is directed to the food, either by those making it or in the quality of the ingredients used. With most fast food we need look no further than the ingredients to have an indication of the quality of the *hado*. Although fast food tastes okay (sometimes) and has the added factor of being 'fast', not many people feel deeply satisfied after a fast food meal. The result is generally a dull feeling. The real reason for this is something simply missing from fast food. That missing ingredient is 'wholesomeness'.

When food is prepared with love, it is appreciated. A wholesome home-cooked meal makes things 'whole'. Love and gratitude seem to make the best ice crystals and have an ability to recover water which has either lost its structure or didn't have it to begin with. When we eat a great meal we feel satisfied and we appreciate the cook. If we have a great meal in a restaurant we might add our compliments to the chef or simply to say 'thank you' for the meal. Food prepared with love and received with gratitude by those eating it brings with it a perfect combination of love and gratitude into food.

It appears, from the research conducted at IHM, that water and food which are heated rapidly have lost their hexagonal structure. Food cooked too quickly forms distorted crystal formations. Hexagonally-structured water in the microwave destroys the hexagonal structure. The same water, when spoken to with words of love and gratitude, recovers somewhat to its original hexagonal form.

Water has an ability to recover but the best approach is to avoid cooking in this way. The same also applies with some of the initial experiments conducted at IHM with rapid freezing of water. When the initial tests were conducted, Masaru Emoto and his researcher tried rapid freezing, using liquid nitrogen as well as state-of-the-art freezing technologies, but with no success. It was only after numerous 'trial and error' experiments that the optimal time frame of three hours of standard slow freezing produced the best results for ice crystals. Both rapid freezing and heating seem to destroy the positive *hado* of food and water.

Perhaps this is due to the method being an entirely unnatural process. A microwave oven has the ability to change the temperature of both food and water very rapidly. The electromagnetic waves of a microwave oven are quite strong, so it is no wonder the results reveal the distortion of water and the ice crystal formations observed from it (see figure 60).

I personally choose not use a microwave oven and do my best to avoid exposure to them in my daily life. I am not suggesting that they are directly harmful to one's health and that you should get rid of your microwave oven. But the images of frozen water under the microscope, after being exposed to the microwave for only fifteen seconds, is food for thought. If just fifteen seconds can destroy the structure of water, imagine what it is doing to the food.

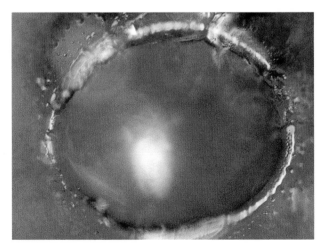

Figure 60. The result of water placed in the microwave oven 15 seconds on high setting

CHAPTER 8

PRACTICAL *HADO* EXERCISES

In this chapter I will share with you a number of practical exercises and meditations to enhance your experience of *hado*, showing how you can utilize these principles on a daily basis to achieve positive results. All of the exercises in this chapter have been 'tested on humans' with great results. Keep in mind that, just because you may be trying these exercises for the first time, you might not be good at them at first. The effectiveness of these exercises is largely fuelled by your trust in your ability to do them.

The first thing to remember is to give these practices your full effort and awareness. It is recommended that you come from a place of 'allowing' and 'being' rather than 'forcing'. With that, you will experience, through the power of your intention and emotions, a powerful transformation which will increase the more you practice. Please enjoy.

Hado smile

Have you ever noticed how a smile can change your day? You could be tired and grumpy, or perhaps you just had an argument with someone. Then, as you walk down the street, a stranger's eyes meet yours and they warmly smile at you. Within a moment you realize you're smiling too. All of the prior feelings vanish and it was as if your grumpy mood never existed.

A sincere smile has the power to transform on many levels. Just like switching on a light in a darkened room, the darkness of your emotions are instantly dispelled. The good thing about smiling is that it works both ways. When you smile at someone they instantly feel better about themselves, life feels easier and a smile brings with it a sense of reassurance.

When we smile, our eyes play a big part - they are intimately connected. The eyes, from an energy perspective, are directly linked with the autonomic nervous system, which itself is divided into sympathetic and parasympathetic systems.

The sympathetic nervous system controls our reactions, whereas the parasympathetic nervous system controls our ability to rest and relax. Smiling with our eyes enables the body to move into a receptive and healing space.

The eyes are also linked with the heart. When we see or hear something beautiful and feel moved, our eyes get wet, and if we are sad or if someone does or says something hurtful, our eyes also get wet. The eyes are linked to the heart. By focusing the energy of a smile through the eyes and inwardly to our hearts, we build a capacity to grow the *hado* of love and gratitude.

Used alone or with other *hado* exercises, *hado* smiling can have a tremendous effect in our lives. At best, smiling consciously throughout your day will cause others to smile and feel better about themselves. At worst, people will wonder what you've been up to! As the saying goes, "Smile and the world smiles with you."

It is interesting to note that a smile forms a natural hexagonal shape in the face. The hexagon's ● left and right sides are the smile which forms in your face, and the bottom of your chin and the upper lip complete the hexagonal shape. Go to a mirror and smile, and you will see the hexagon formed in your face. Perhaps this is the reason a smile is so attractive: it forms a natural beauty of nature for others to see.

As we have seen in examples of ice crystals, the hexagonal structure is the core structure of the most beautiful and balanced ice crystal formations, such as love and gratitude (figure 61). Smiling forms a beautiful hexagon, the divine principle of sacred geometry written all over your face.

The following exercise has its origins in the Taoist masters of ancient China. It is a direct way to experience the healing benefits from the practice of the 'inner smile'.

Begin by finding a comfortable position, either seated in a chair or on a cushion. Do not lie down (as you may end up falling asleep). Be comfortable and relaxed. Begin by stating your intention that you are now going to use your time for the *hado* smiling practice.

Gently close your eyes and begin by stilling your mind. Become aware of your breath as it comes and goes at the tip of your nose. Let all thoughts and concerns of the past go, without holding on to any of them, neither by pushing them away. Simply be here and now, being aware of your breath as it comes and goes. As you connect with your breath, become aware of your body and consciously relax. You may notice that you have tension in a part of your body: imagine that, with each exhalation, all of your tension is effortlessly melting away. Become aware of your muscles softening and, as you do, feel yourself becoming more accustomed to feeling light and peaceful. You can even repeat the word 'relax' three times with each exhalation.

Now begin to smile. Even if you don't feel like it, smile and tune into the feeling and the shape created by the smile in your face. As you smile, now imagine that the energy of the smile is radiating up into your eyes. Imagine your eyes are now smiling, as you would smile to a loved one. Now that your eyes and mouth are smiling, notice how you are feeling.

Keeping this awareness of the eyes and mouth smiling, imagine that this radiant energy is now streaming down from your eyes to your heart. Fill your heart with this pure energy and imagine your heart smiling with love and gratitude. Now your heart, eyes and mouth are smiling. Tune in to this feeling and the energy of the smile. Begin to spread this feeling out into the various areas of your body and inner organs.

Imagine that your face and jaw are filled with the energy of the smile. You can imagine the energy of the smile spreading out from your face as a soft radiant white light. Now fill your neck and throat with the energy of the smile. Follow the energy of your smile to your lungs, your liver, kidneys, adrenals, pancreas and spleen. Continue to smile down to your stomach, to the small and large intestines and the rectum and genitals (are you smiling yet?). Then turn your smiling energy to your spine, moving from the top vertebrae to the base, one by one. Next, run your awareness to smiling down to your arms and legs. Imagine your entire body is filled with the energy and warmth of your smile.

Continue to reside in the awareness of this experience for as long as you like. To finish the exercise, gently open your eyes, still smiling, and share this positive *hado* as you go about your day.

Once you have completed the practice, notice how you are feeling. Do you feel more at ease, peaceful and relaxed? Repeat the exercise daily until smiling becomes a habit you are strongly addicted to. This is a worthwhile addiction.

Hado prayer

Depending upon your background, prayer may be familiar to you or a completely foreign concept. Regardless of what you know or do not know, allow yourself in this exercise to drop your preconceptions and follow along with it. *Hado* prayer is a practice of cultivating intention and generating positive emotions in prayer. It cultivates a 'good heart', which can be brought into any prayer or wish.

The following exercise offers a method for praying consciously and has five distinct stages. The first stage involves stilling your mind and relaxation. The second stage is a prayer, acknowledging what you are grateful for. The third stage is a prayer or request for yourself. The fourth stage is a prayer or request for others. The fifth and final stage is a prayer of giving thanks once more, but this time for the desired result.

Begin by finding a comfortable position, either seated in a chair or on a cushion. Do not lie down (as you may end up falling asleep). Be comfortable and relaxed. Begin by stating your intention that you are now going to use this time for *hado* prayer.

Gently close your eyes and begin by stilling your mind, by becoming aware of your breath as it comes and goes at the tip of your nose. Let go of all the thoughts and concerns of the past, without holding on to any of them, neither pushing them away. Simply be here and now, being aware of your breath as it comes and goes naturally. As you connect with your breath, become aware of your body and consciously relax. You may notice that you have tension in a part of your body. Imagine that, with each exhalation, all of your tension is effortlessly melting away. Become aware of your muscles softening and, as you do, feel yourself becoming more accustomed to feeling light and peaceful. You can even repeat the word 'relax' three times with each exhalation, if you like.

Now focus your awareness in your heart center in the middle of your chest. When we offer our prayers from our heart (instead of our head), a new kind of prayer is born – it is a prayer from the heart, of love and gratitude.

Become aware of this place and imagine you are breathing into your heart. As you do, you may imagine a feeling of warmth and love. Build up this quality of love and gratitude until it feels real to you in this moment. As you feel this experience of love and gratitude, begin to smile (if you are not doing so already). As you smile, feel the energy of the smile in your heart, as if your heart is smiling throughout the entire practice.

From this place, ask yourself the question: "What is it that I am grateful for?"

Contemplate this question for a few moments without answering. When you feel ready, allow the prayer to speak to you. Let the words of gratitude spill forth, either silently or aloud.

Your prayer may start like this: "Creator, the spirit in all things, I give thanks for…" Continue to speak your heart's gratitude until you come to a place of completion. You may wish to acknowledge outer things, such as the people in your life or situations you are grateful for. Then you may move to giving thanks for your inner qualities. Remember to focus only on giving thanks. If you come to a place where your mind goes blank, become aware of your grateful heart and of your breathing. From this place, you may find that more words of thanks come.

Once you feel your heart has spoken its words of gratitude, acknowledging the gifts you have, both inner and outer, then consciously still your mind once again.

From this place, ask yourself the question: "What is it that I require for myself?" Contemplate this question. When you feel ready, allow the prayer to speak to you. Let the words of your request spill forth.

Your personal prayer of request may start like this: "Creator, the spirit in all things, I request..." Continue to speak your heart's requests. Once you feel your heart has spoken its words of request, consciously still your mind once again.

Now move your attention to your prayer of request for others. You may wish

to start like this: "Creator, the spirit in all things, may your divinity bless…"
Continue to speak your heart's requests. Once you feel your heart has spoken its
words of request for others, consciously still your mind once again.

The final stage is to imagine that all of your prayers are received. You may
think to yourself: "I now give thanks to the Creator for receiving these requests
and give thanks for their answers." You may imagine that all your requests are
coming back into you in the form of radiant pure light, streaming into your body
from all directions and into your heart. Imagine this light and these blessings are
now filling your entire body. You are now completely filled with this grace of
divinity. With a grateful heart, reside for as long as you wish in this experience.

When you are ready, gently open your eyes and come out of the practice, carrying the essence of your experience into your day.

Depending upon your religions background, you may wish to insert your
deity of choice, or you may pray simply to your divine self, or to the divine intelligence of the universe. For those who do not wish to pray to gods or deities,
some alternatives I have found useful include:

May Divine Intelligence bless my life with…
May the blessings of the Universe…
May that which is true…
May the heart of compassion and love…
May my higher self bless…
May the love and gratitude of my heart bless…

It matters not whether we consider this higher principle to be within, outside or
both. It matters that we take time to give thanks and to feel gratitude.

Hado prayer is ideally offered in the morning before you rise, and during the
evening before you sleep. In the morning you can place more emphasis on
putting out to the universe what you want to attract. In the evening you can place
more emphasis on giving thanks to the universe for all that are grateful for. Use
hado prayer as much as you desire. You can use *hado* prayer anytime, anywhere.

Just close your eyes and go through the five steps with a smile on your face.

Affirmation of self-love exercise

The following practice for cultivating self-love is wonderful way to gain a more wholesome relationship with yourself. The more we can appreciate and love ourselves, the more we can love and appreciate others. This practice is not designed to swell our ego: it is done to acknowledge and love the truth and beauty inside us.

To begin the practice, sit yourself in front of a full length mirror and quiet your mind. Once you feel more comfortable doing this exercise, you may even wish to do this practice naked.

Become aware of your breath, as it comes and goes at the tip of your nose, and let all of your thoughts and ideas about yourself just go by. This time your eyes are open to observe your beautiful reflection.

Now observe yourself and begin by looking into your eyes. As you gaze into your eyes, become aware of your heart center. As you breathe, imagine you are breathing light into your heart and, as you do so, it begins to warm with a sense of gratitude. From this place, acknowledge the beauty which is you. Say out loud the following affirmation to yourself:

I am a true aspect of divinity. All that I am derives from this wellspring of love. I give thanks for this recognition. I respect and love myself for all that I am, now and into the future.

Repeat this affirmation three times.

After saying these words to yourself, become aware of how you feel. Do you notice a difference? Next, become aware of your body. Continue to look into your eyes and say the following affirmation:

My body is a true aspect of divinity. My body and all its senses are derived from this wellspring of love. I give thanks for this recognition and respect. I love my body for all that it is, now and into the future.

Repeat this affirmation three times. After speaking these words to yourself, become aware of how you feel. Next, become aware of your heart center, continuing to look into your eyes, and say the following affirmation:

My heart is a true aspect of divinity. My heart is derived from this wellspring of love. I give thanks for this recognition and I respect and love my heart for all that it is, now and into the future.

Repeat this affirmation three times.

Finish the exercise by being aware of how you feel and notice how you feel about yourself. You may find there was some resistance. You may feel relaxed or more peaceful. Whatever the outcome, it is desirable to repeat this exercise daily. The more your practice self-love, the more you will train your mind to become what you affirm on a very real level.

In figure 55 we see how water responds to the words 'self-love'. The inner core seems to be radiating light outwards in all directions, forming a beautiful ice crystal. It speaks volumes about the result of self-love. Genuine self-love is something the whole world sees.

Figure 61. Distilled water shown the words 'love and gratitude'

Aligning the water in your body with love and gratitude

Of all the thousands of ice crystals that have been recorded, most people agree that the ice crystal of love and gratitude (figure 61) is one of the most beautiful and balanced formations. If the *hado* of love and gratitude can do this to water, imagine what love and gratitude can do for us. If we look at ourselves as constituted mostly as water, aligning with the *hado* of love and gratitude is a direct and positive way to raise our vibration.

The following meditation practice is designed to align our body and mind to the *hado* of love and gratitude. When meditating in this way we align the water in our body to a vibration resonating with love and gratitude.

Sit in a comfortable position and place your hands in your lap. Close your eyes, relax and breathe steadily and easily. Begin by directing your awareness to the meditation and affirm your intention to activate the *hado* of love and gratitude in your body.

Now direct your awareness to your heart center in the middle of your chest. Become aware of a fine point of light in this place. This light symbolizes your true unlimited potential.

Now move your awareness to the top of your head. At a distance you could easily reach above your head, imagine that a small point of light emerges. Like observing the first star in the sky at dusk, imagine this small star above your head, symbolizing all of the blessings and purity of the universe.

As you become aware of the two lights, in your heart and above your head, like small stars dancing in space, you notice the star above your head now melts down through your head and meets with the light in your heart center. As soon as the two lights meet, they melt together and the ice crystal of love and gratitude forms in your heart. Experience the depth of love and gratitude in your heart and build up these feelings.

Notice that, from this singular ice crystal of love and gratitude, a second one now appears. From two, another two appear. From the four, another four appear. Now there are eight, then 16, then 32, 64, 128 and so forth.

Imagine the ice crystals continue to multiply and radiate out in all directions, filling your entire body with hundreds and thousands of love and gratitude ice crystals. Instead of feeling cold, experience your body's water, your blood and every fiber of your being, being flooded with the gentle warmth of love and gratitude. These thousands of ice crystals now multiply into hundred of thousands. Imagine your whole being is transformed into the essence of love and gratitude.

Any areas of illness, disease or imbalance are instantly transformed when touched by the love and gratitude crystals. Imagine your entire body is filled with light. Now all of the ice crystals dissolve and you are left with a positive energy of love and gratitude. Stay with this experience for as long as you like.

Once you feel that you can no long hold this experience, gently bring your awareness back to the outer world. Slowly open your eyes and feel the radiant and pure vibration moving throughout your entire body.

Love and gratitude blessing practice for others

The following practice is for transforming aversion and for blessing all beings everywhere with love and gratitude. This practice helps to subdue pride and cultivates a generous spirit. When we focus our intention of sharing love and gratitude with others we really assist our personal growth. When we grow, we can truly be a light unto others and benefit them in lasting ways.

We begin by approaching the practice in the same way as above, aligning the water in our body with love and gratitude, so this practice can if you wish be added to the end of the previous one.

Sit in a comfortable position and place your hands in your lap. Close your eyes, relax and breathe steadily and easily. Begin by directing your awareness to the meditation and affirm your intention to activate the *hado* of love and gratitude in your body and extend this to sharing the love and gratitude blessing practice for others.

Now direct your awareness to your heart center in the middle of your chest. Become aware of a fine point of light in this place. This light symbolizes your true unlimited potential. Now move your awareness to the top of your head. At a distance you could easily reach, imagine that a small point of light emerges above your head. Like observing the first star in the sky at dusk, imagine this small star above your head, symbolizing all of the blessings and purity of the universe.

As you become aware of the two lights, like small stars dancing in space, notice that the star above your head now melts down through your head and meets with the light in your heart center. As soon as the two lights meet, they melt together and the ice crystal of love and gratitude forms in your heart. Experience now the depth of love and gratitude in your heart and build up these feelings.

Notice that, from this singular ice crystal of love and gratitude, a second one appears. From two, another two appear. From the four, another four appear. Now there are eight, then 16, then 32, 64, 128 and so forth. Imagine that the ice crystals continue to multiply and now radiate out in all directions, filling your entire body with hundreds and thousands of love and gratitude ice crystals. Instead of feeling cold, experience your body's water, your blood and every fiber of your being, flooded with the gentle warmth of love and gratitude. These thousands of ice crystals now multiply into hundred of thousands. Imagine that your whole being is transformed into the essence of love and gratitude.

Any areas of illness; disease or imbalance is instantly transformed when touched by the love and gratitude crystals. Imagine your entire body is filled with light. Unable to contain the boundless love and gratitude, this energy now begins to pour from the pores of your skin and out into space.

Imagine now that all beings everywhere are attracted to your radiant energy and are now gathered around you. Imagine that, to your left, your mother stands as you know or remember her. To your right your father stands as you know or remember him. Behind you, imagine that all of those who you hold dear and all loved ones now stand. In front of you, imagine all those who you have challenges with and all who you feel an aversion to are there before you.

Unlimited love and gratitude now shines out from your body. It touches your mother, your father, all those who you love and lastly all those who you feel aversion to. Once touched by these lights, they are instantly blessed and transformed.

We now become aware of our bodies again, feeling whole, blessed and radiant. With this we end the meditation, bringing back into the world the feeling of love and gratitude, knowing that we didn't gain something new but rather experienced the true essence of what was always there. Stay with this experience for as long as you like.

Once you feel that you can no longer hold this experience, gently bring your awareness back to the outer world. Slowly open your eyes and feel the radiant and pure vibration moving throughout your entire body.

Creating and blessing *hado* water

Creating *hado* water is as simple as taking a marker and writing the words 'love and thanks' on a clear bottle, or setting a glass of pure water upon these words. Alternatively you can take pure water and set it on an ice crystal image or any photo which has a positive vibration. See figure 62.

Figure 62. Filtered water placed upon words and images with positive *Hado*

Some natural therapists I know place a glass of water on a photograph of a particular flower known for its vibrational healing properties. Others place a glass on an image of a deity, mantra or an image of a holy teacher or place. This alone can have a dramatic effect on the vibrational quality of the water you drink.

However, if you wish to really change and make positively-charged water with your intention, the following practice works wonders. I have conducted this meditation with hundreds of people who have never performed any such practice, all with amazing results.

To highlight the effectiveness of this practice, we usually conduct the blessing as an experiment in which we use two glasses of ordinary tap water. One glass acts as the control sample and the other is the one where the person focuses their intention upon it. When conducting the experiment in *hado* workshops, I ask the person who has charged their water to offer it to the person next to them, thus ruling out personal projections regarding the change in quality and taste. Every time I have conducted this experiment, more than 95% of participants can actually taste the difference in the *hado* water when sharing it with others.

If you wish to try this yourself, feel free to use tap water. Ideally it is best to start with pure filtered water, as you have an opportunity to increase the already established purity and embellish it with the *hado* frequency.

To begin the water blessing practice, sit in a comfortable position and place your hands on either side of the glass of water that you wish to bless with *hado*. Your hands are held at heart level in the middle of your chest with your hands either side, as illustrated in figure 63. Close your eyes and breathe steadily and easily.

Affirm your wish to activate the *hado* frequency for blessing and creating *hado* water. Now direct your awareness to your heart center in the middle of your chest. Become aware of a fine point of light in this place. This light symbolizes your true unlimited potential.

Now move your awareness to the top of your head. At a distance you could easily reach, imagine that a small point of light emerges. Like observing the first star in the sky at dusk, imagine that this small star above your head symbolizes all of the blessings and purity of the universe.

As you become aware of the two lights, like small stars dancing in space, notice how the star above your head now melts down through your head and meets with the light in your heart center. As soon as the two lights meet, they melt together and a great sphere of radiant light forms in your heart. Imagine that, from this sphere of light, there emanates an infinite source of love and gratitude. This *hado* energy of love and gratitude now radiates down both arms and into the palms where the glass of water is being held.

From the center of your chest where the radiant light sphere resides, the light now shines out and melts into the water between your hands. Imagine that this pure energy also streams out from your palms into the water.

As you continue to fill the glass of water with this energy, both from the palms of your hands and from the sphere in your heart center, become aware that a similar radiant sphere has formed and is now suspended in the center of the glass of water. It now begins to radiate love and gratitude outwards in all directions. This light continues to stream directly from your heart and hands. Feel the healing energy of love and gratitude as it streams into the water, blessing it with the *hado* of love and gratitude.

Now repeat the following affirmation, either silently or aloud, three times: "We thank you water; we love you water, may our love and blessings fill you."

Imagine the light in the water goes to every direction so it becomes inseparable from the radiant sphere. Finish the practice once you feel the body of water is full of energy.

Now your *hado* water is ready to use. A few drops can be placed on your palms before you commence any healing or bodywork, or it can be added to medicines, or the water can be taken by your friends and family when ill. It can be placed in a spray container and sprayed on your skin, or in a room to purify it, or combined with essences and other natural medicines.

This practice is very effective and will bring results you can taste. If you wish to create a greater volume of *hado* water, such as by using a water dispenser like the ones used in home or office, simply do the practice as before and sit in front of the container, as illustrated in figure 64.

If you have blessed a larger container of water, always ensure your *hado* water does not become emptied. When the water is getting low, add new pure water and re-do the blessing practice. With continued practice the water and container become more and more powerful as a tool for generating *hado* water.

You can also place your *hado* water on a coaster of an ice crystal image to keep energizing the water. It is also useful to talk to your water container as you pass by.

Every time I pass by my water container I say, "Hello, water" or "Thank you, water" or "Aren't you beautiful?" or "You're cute!". Whichever way you look at it, the more positive attention you give to water, the more you increase the positive *hado* in it. Of course, if you work in an office your co-workers many think you are a bit strange. An alternative is to smile at the water or simply think the words to it. The result is much the same.

Showing appreciation for food

Cultivating the emotion of appreciation for food is a wonderful way to enhance

its natural qualities. This makes a lot of sense, as you will then be ingesting these same qualities which can only be useful in your personal development.

The art of blessing food is an ancient practice. It is practiced in almost all religions. In my own experience, Buddhism, Shamanism and Christianity all have rituals for blessing food. For Christians the blessing of food is (or at least, was) commonplace. Brought up as a Christian, I recall blessing my meals each day, but not with a true awareness with which I would be

Figure 63. Hands held around a glass of water for creating *Hado* water

Figure 64. Hands held around a large container of water for creating *Hado* water

increasing the vibratory level of my mother's cooking (which I recall was in need of some blessings). When blessing food therefore, we should not just go through the motions without involving our feelings. The more we can consciously bring in feelings of love and gratitude, the greater the blessing will be.

To bless food or water requires a sincerely felt sense of love and gratitude. If we simply offer a blessing with no real motivation the benefit will be minimal, as our human intention plays a large part in affecting a positive outcome.

When dining out, if you have no idea who prepared the food, you can do a short exercise to bless your food, which need not be a formal ritual. This has the added bonus of not attracting funny looks from fellow patrons. The following is quick and simple exercise which was given to me by my Buddhist master. I often do this exercise when eating out.

Before eating a meal, place your hands either side of the plate or bowl. In your mind give thanks for the meal and make wishes that this food will benefit you in every way. Next imagine that enlightened beings and forms gather above and around your meal. You can imagine these as tiny points of light, like stars containing all wholesome energies. Lift up your plate an inch from the table in a gesture of offering (or you can imagine lifting the plate, if you wish) and, in response to this pure offering, all of these enlightened qualities now transform into rainbow-colored light and fall into the meal and are absorbed by the food. Say "Thank you for your blessings", either silently or out loud. Proceed to eat your meal with a sense of gratitude.

This small practice takes about ten seconds and most people won't think you are crazy if they see you lifting your plate from the table for a few seconds.

The Grand Invocation

Masaru Emoto wrote the following invocation with the sincere wish that all those who encountered it would use it to increase *hado* and align the invocation it in the minds and hearts of all humanity. It is an invocation or prayer to call forth a new era of harmony, which is something our world needs now more than ever.

The invocation is traditionally read in Japanese, but for those of us who do not read Japanese, I have written a translation in English so that the meaning is felt when spoken. The more we all align with this wish for humanity, the more we will become aligned as one people.

It is like a still pond. The message of water is like a stone thrown into it, and the movement of a new consciousness spreading throughout the world are the ripples spreading out in all directions. May this invocation touch your life and the lives of all those who share it. Please use it.

The Grand Invocation (Japanese: *Dai Dan Gen*)

In Japanese: *Uchuu no mugen no chikara ga korikotte. Makoto no dqiwa no miyo ga narinata.*

A literal translation: universe, eternal, energy, crystallized, true, great harmony, era, has come.

This is a literal translation, but for it to read more easily, I have re-worded the invocation in the following manner:

May the eternal energy of the universe be crystallized in truth here and now, for the era of great harmony has come.

So what does this invocation really mean? The following is a more detailed description. The first part:

May the eternal energy of the universe...

This first part speaks to us about that which never dies, the unchanging universal principle – the *hado* of the universe and the energy which gives life and meaning to all.

...be crystallized in truth here and now...

May the universal and eternal principle manifest upon this Earth in the hearts and minds of everyone, here and now. It is time to know and embrace this universal law which underpins the very nature of reality.

...for the era of great harmony has come.

The era is now. It is a prayer and a wish to bring this new level of awareness into a world which is crying out for harmony. We see in the world the manifestation of disharmony, and the remedy or cure for this is the opposite vibration, a great harmony. By thinking in this way, as if it has already come, we call this great harmony to us.

APPENDIX

The following article has been reprinted for publication with the kind permission of EXPLORE: The Journal of Science and Healing, V2 (5): 2006; 2:408-411. © Elsevier Inc. 2006.

Double-Blind Test of
the Effects of Distant Intention on Water Crystal Formation

Conducted by Dean Radin PhD (DR) and Gail Hayssen (GH) of the Noetic Sciences Institute, Petaluma, CA, USA, and Masaru Emoto (ME) and Takashige Kizu BA (TK), of IHM Research Institute, Tokyo, Japan.

The hypothesis that water 'treated' with intention can affect ice crystals formed from that water was pilot tested under double-blind conditions. A group of approximately 2,000 people in Tokyo focused positive intentions toward water samples located inside an electromagnetically shielded room in California. That group was unaware of similar water samples set aside in a different location as controls. Ice crystals formed from both sets of water samples were blindly identified and photographed by an analyst, and the resulting images were blindly assessed for aesthetic appeal by 100 independent judges. Results indicated that crystals from the treated water were given higher scores for aesthetic appeal than those from the control water, lending support to the hypothesis.

INTRODUCTION

Experiments over the past four decades have investigated whether intention affects properties of water. This question is of interest to complementary and alternative medicine research, and especially for therapies involving intention, because the adult human body consists of approximately 70% water.[1] The question has been studied by comparing the effects of intentionally 'treated' water versus untreated control water on the germination and growth of plants, including barley, [2-4] wheat,[5] rye,[6] beans,[7] cress,[8] radishes,[9] and lettuce.[10] Other properties of water that have been examined include rate of cooling,[11] molecular bonding as reflected by infrared spectra alterations,[12-16] Raman spectroscopy,[17] scattered laser light,[18] and pH level.[19] Although formal meta-analyses have not been performed on these studies, overall, the experiments provide evidence suggesting that various properties of water may be influenced by intention.

Interest in this topic has been rekindled recently by claims suggesting that intentionally influenced water can be detected by examining ice crystals formed from samples of that water.[20,21] The specific claim is that positive intentions tend to produce symmetric, well-formed, aesthetically pleasing crystals, and negative intentions tend to produce asymmetric, poorly formed, unattractive crystals.

As of this study, no experimental replications of these claims have been published in peer-reviewed journals, so most critiques have assumed that the simplest explanation for the claimed results is either biased selection of crystal images or selective reporting of results or both.[22] This paper reports a pilot investigation of the crystal formation hypothesis to test the claim under double-blind conditions.

METHODS
Water Sample Preparation
In preparation for the experiment, the second author (GH) purchased four plastic bottles of Fiji brand commercial bottled water (Los Angeles, CA). This brand was selected because, unlike many other bottled waters, after the Fiji label was removed, the plastic bottle contained no words, symbols or other shapes embossed in the plastic. The first author (DR) randomly assigned the bottles with labels A through D (using a tossed die) and, with GH, he selected two of those bottles to be the 'treated' samples (randomly selected as A and B); the remaining two bottles were set aside as controls (C and D).

The treatment bottles were placed inside a double-steel walled, electromagnetically shielded room (Series 81 Solid Cell; Lindgren/ETS, Cedar Park, TX) at the Institute of Noetic Sciences (IONS) in Petaluma, California. This room was used primarily as a convenient, limited-access location in which to place the bottles during the remote treatment period. The control bottles were placed in separate cardboard boxes and stored on a desk in a quiet location on another floor of the building that housed the shielded room. DR and GH did not inform the third or fourth authors (ME or TK) about the existence of the control bottles until after the treatment period was completed.

A digital photo of the two treatment bottles in the shielded chamber was e-mailed to ME and TK in Tokyo to be used as a visual aid for a group that would later be directing their intentions toward those bottles. The treatment and control bottles were maintained at approximately the same temperatures and were handled approximately the same length of time.

Treatment

On November 16, 2005, ME led a group of approximately 2,000 people in Tokyo in a prayer of gratitude directed toward the water in the IONS laboratory some 5,000 miles away. Masaru Emoto showed the audience where the IONS laboratory was located in relationship to Tokyo by using a sequence of images from the Google Earth global mapping application (Mountain View, CA). Next, he showed the digital picture of the bottles inside the shielded chamber with the words of an intentional 'prayer for water' overlaid on the photo. After explaining the photo and purpose of the experiment, ME led the group in speaking aloud the words of the prayer. This lasted approximately five minutes.

Analysis

The day after the conference, DR and GH retrieved all four bottles and wrapped them in identical sheets of aluminum foil and bubble wrap, placed each bottle in a separate box labeled A through D as appropriate, and mailed the four boxes to ME's laboratory. (The treatment and control bottles were in their separate locations for approximately 36 hours before being brought together again for packaging.) The bubble wrap and aluminum foil were used to provide a rudimentary shield against sudden shocks, ambient light and electromagnetic fields that might have impinged on the bottles while *en route* to Japan. Each box was packaged separately to avoid the possibility that treated bottles might influence the control bottles through close proximity. After mailing the boxes, DR and GH informed ME and TK about the two control bottles, but they were not told the conditions of the four bottles to ensure that their analysis would be conducted blindly.

Upon receiving the four boxes, TK examined water samples from each bottle according to the following procedure:

1. For each bottle, approximately 0.5 ml of water was placed into each of 50 Petri dishes, and a lid was placed on each dish.

2. Each dish was then placed into a freezer maintained at -25 to -30°C for a minimum of 3 hours.

3. TK later removed the dishes from the freezer and, in a walk-in refrigerator (maintained at -5°C), he examined the apex of each resulting ice drop for a crystal using a stereo optical microscope. Previous experience with ice drops formed under these conditions indicated that the apex was the location where crystals were most likely to form. Crystals were defined as hexagonal shapes.

4. If a crystal was observed at the apex (not all ice drops formed discernable crystals), TK photographed it at either -100 or -200 magnification, depending on the size of the crystal.

5. All resulting photographs, from all four bottles, were then e-mailed to DR.

RESULTS

Analysis of Crystals

DR received a total of 40 photographs: 12 crystals were from bottle A, 12 from B, 7 from C, and 9 from D. Bottles A and B were the treated bottles, thus slightly more crystals were identified in the treated condition. To assess the aesthetic appeal of these 40 crystals, a group of 100 volunteers were recruited over the Internet to blindly and independently rate each crystal, one at a time, on a scale from zero to six, where zero meant 'not beautiful' and six meant 'very beautiful'. (The ratings were collected via a website programmed in Perl/CGI by the first author.) Beautiful crystals were defined as symmetric, aesthetically-pleasing shapes.

The order in which each image was presented to each judge (via a web page) was independently randomized. In addition, the image titles (eg: '2.jpg', '3.jpg') were assigned random numbers so the condition could not be inferred by examining the name of the crystal image and the condition (treated vs control) from which each crystal was formed was not indicated, and no feedback was provided at the end of the assessment exercise to prevent judges from learning which images corresponded to which conditions. The planned analysis was based on the first 100 judges to complete ratings of all 40 crystals, for a total of 4,000 contributed ratings.

Comparison of Ratings

Comparison of the mean ratings assigned to the images showed that the crystals from the treated water were rated significantly higher for aesthetic appeal than the crystals from the control water.

DISCUSSION

This pilot study was designed to test the most plausible conventional explanation for the crystal formation claim: the presence of subjective biases. To eliminate these biases, the person taking photos of the crystals (TK) and the aesthetic raters of those crystals were both blind to the treatment versus control conditions. The results were consistent with the hypothesis that water treated with pleasant intentions would result in more pleasing crystal shapes. If this effect was not due to obvious subjective biases, then what else might have accounted for the results?

Could the image assessment process have introduced a systematic rating bias? This question arises because each rater examined 40 crystal photos without prior training on the meaning of 'aesthetically beautiful'. If the sequence in which raters observed these images was in a fixed order, then this might well have introduced an artifact. However, this possibility was specifically prevented by presenting the images in a newly randomized order for each rater, thus averaging out potential sequential effects.

Another concern may be that the scales used to assess beauty, which were based on ordinal rather than interval measurements, violated the t test assumption of an underlying normal distribution. This potential problem was ameliorated by using scores averaged across 100 raters, but parametric assumptions can be completely avoided by using a nonparametric statistic.[23] The method we used compared the observed mean difference in ratings between treated and control crystal images to the same mean difference determined after randomly reassigning which images belonged to the treated and control conditions. The original mean difference was larger than 999 out of 1,000 randomly reassigned differences, thus the associated P value was P -.001, virtually identical to the results of the t test.

One might ask whether a new group of raters would replicate the initial results. This was tested by examining the results provided by 100 additional raters. The resulting t test was t (38 df) - 3.11, P - .002, confirming the original findings.

Perhaps the treated and control bottles were handled differently (say, with more fingerprints on the treated bottles), and the analyst (TK) detected those differences and was subsequently biased. Anticipating such artifacts, investigators DR and GH took care to ensure that the four bottles were physically handled the same way and then packaged identically. A related question is whether the treated and control environments might have differed in important ways. The treated bottles were in an electromagnetically shielded room during the treatment period, but the control bottles were not. In addition, that shielded room had been used exclusively for intention-related experiments for several years prior to this experiment. It is conceivable that purported 'space conditioning' effects, as reported in previous intention studies, or simply differences in exposure to ambient electromagnetic radiation, may have played a role in the present outcome.[18,24]

Future studies would also benefit by assessing photographs of the apexes of all available ice drops rather than just those with crystalline shapes because this would eliminate all subjective (albeit blind) assessments on the part of the analyst. The Petri dishes from different water samples might also be randomly distributed inside the freezer to avoid any inherent temperature or position differences, and more objective methods of assessing the aesthetic properties of the crystals could be employed.[25,26]

There are at least three unconventional alternatives that might explain the observed effects. One is that the intentional source was not the audience in Tokyo but rather DR and GH. This possibility cannot be excluded but, although these investigators were open to the hypothesis, neither held strong expectations about the experimental outcome. A second possibility is that the water was not altered at all, but rather the bottles were randomly assigned by DR and GH to the two conditions that would later result in a fortuitous differential effect or that TK fortuitously decided to take photos that would ultimately result in the observed outcome or both.

Such anomalous assignment effects, formalized as 'Decision Augmentation Theory',[27] require the ability to unconsciously sense and act upon future possibilities, ie, a form of precognition. A third possibility is that the intentions of future observers (including readers of this article) *retroactively* influenced the water. Although this explanation may seem outrageous, there is experimental evidence suggesting that such time-reversed effects may exist.[28]

In conclusion, the present pilot results are consistent with a number of previous studies suggesting that intention may be able to influence the structure of water. Future replications should concentrate on eliminating all conceivable conventional artifacts, and protocols should be employed that can help discriminate among the various unconventional explanations.

REFERENCES

1. Sheng HP, Huggins RA. A review of body composition studies with emphasis on total body water and fat. *Am J Clin Nutr.* 1979;32:630- 647.

2. Grad B. A telekinetic effect on plant growth. *Int J Parapsych.*1963; 5:117-133.

3. Grad B. A telekinetic effect on plant growth. II. Experiments involving treatment of saline in stoppered bottles. *Int J Parapsych.* 1964; 6: 473-498.

4. Saklani A. Follow-up studies of PK effects on plant growth. *J Soc Psych Res.* 1992; 58:258-265.

5. Saklani A. Preliminary tests for psi-ability in shamans of Garhwal Himalaya. *J Soc Psych Res.* 1988; 55:60-70.

6. Munson RJ. The effects of PK on rye seeds. *J Parapsych.* 1979; 43:43.

7. Barrington MR. Bean growth promotion pilot experiment. *Proc Soc Psych Res.* 1982; 56:302-304.

8. Scofield AM, Hodges RD. Demonstration of a healing effect in the laboratory using a simple plant model. *J Soc Psych Res.* 1991; 57:321-343.

9. Lenington S. Effect of holy water on the growth of radish plants. *Psych Rep.* 1979; 45:381-382.

10. Roney-Dougal SM, Solfvin J. Field study of enhancement effect on lettuce seeds: their germination rate, growth and health. *J Soc Psych Res.* 2004; 66:129- 142.

11. Chauvin R. "Built upon water" psychokinesis and water cooling: an exploratory study. *J Soc Psych Res.* 1988; 55:10-15.

12. Schwartz SA, De Mattei RJ, Brame EG, Spottiswoode SJP. Infrared spectra alteration in water proximate to the palms of therapeutic practitioners. *Subtle Energies Energy Med.* 1990; 1:43-72.

13. Dean D. *An Examination of Intra-Red and Ultra-Violet Techniques to Test for Changes in Water Following the Laying-On-Of-Hands.* [Doctoral dissertation]. University Microfilms International, No. 8408650. Saybrook Institute; 1983: 111-115.

14. Fenwick P, Hopkins R. An examination of the effect of healing on water. *J*

Soc Psych Res. 1986; 53:387-390.

15. Dean D. Infrared measurements of healer treated water. In: Roll WG, Beloff J, White RA, eds. *Research in Parapsychology 1982.* Metuchen, NJ: Scarecrow Press; 1983: 100-101.

16. Grad B, Dean D. Independent confirmation of infrared healer effects. In: White RA, Broughton RS, eds. *Research in Parapsychology 1983.* Metuchen, NJ: Scarecrow Press; 1984: 81-83.

17. Yan X, Lu F, Jiang H, *et al.* Certain physical manifestation and effects of external qi of Yan Xin life science technology. *J Sci Expl.* 2002; 16:381-411.

18. Pyatnitsky LN, Fonkin VA. Human consciousness influence on water structure. *J Sci Expl.* 1995; 9:89-105.

19. Dibble WE, Tiller WA. Electronic device-mediated pH changes in water. *J Sci Expl.* 1999; 13:155-176.

20. Emoto M. Healing with water. *J Altern Complement Med.* 2004; 10:19-21.

21. Emoto M. *The Hidden Messages in Water.* Hillsboro, OR: Beyond Words Publishing; 2004.

22. Matthews R. Water: The quantum elixir. *New Scientist.* April 8, 2006: 32-37.

23. Davison AC, Hinkley DV. *Bootstrap Methods and Their Application.* (Cambridge Series in Statistical and Probabilistic Mathematics, No 1). Cambridge, UK: Cambridge University Press; 1997.

24. Radin DI, Taft R, Yount G. Possible effects of healing intention on cell cultures and truly random events. *J Altern Complement Med.* 2004; 10:103-112.

25. Laviea T, Tractinsky N. Assessing dimensions of perceived visual aesthetics of web sites. *Int J Hum Comp Stud.* 2004; 60:269-298.

26. Gobster PH, Chenoweth RE. The dimensions of aesthetic preference: a quantitative analysis. *J Environ Manage.* 1989; 29:47-72.

27. May EC, Utts JM, Spottiswoode SJP. Decision augmentation theory: Towards a model of anomalous mental phenomena. *J Parapsych.* 1995; 59:195-220.

28. Braud W. Wellness implications of retroactive intentional influence: exploring an outrageous hypothesis. *Altern Ther Health Med.* 2000; 6:37-48.

ABOUT THE AUTHOR

Lawrence Ellyard is a certified *Hado* Instructor trained by Masura Emoto. He is the co-founder and director of *Hado Institute Australia*. He is a board member of the International *Hado* Instructors and currently lives in Australia. *The Spirit of Water* is his sixth book.

About Masaru Emoto

Masaru Emoto was born in Yokohama in July 1943. He is a graduate of the Yokohama Municipal University's department of humanities and sciences with a focus on International Relations. In 1986 he established the IHM (International Health Medical) Corporation in Tokyo. In October of 1992 he received certification from the Open International University as a Doctor of Alternative Medicine. Subsequently he was introduced to the concept of micro-cluster water in the US and Magnetic Resonance Analysis technology. The quest thus began to discover the mystery of water.

He undertook extensive research of water around the planet not so much as a scientific researcher but more from the perspective of an original thinker. At length he realized that it was in the frozen crystal form that water showed us its true nature through. He has gained worldwide acclaim through his groundbreaking research and discovery that water is deeply connected to our individual and collective consciousness.

He is the author of the best-selling books *Messages from Water*, *The Hidden Messages in Water*, and *The True Power of Water*. He is a long-time advocate for peace in relation to water. He is currently the head of the IHM General Research Institute and President Emeritus of the International Water for Life Foundation, a Not for Profit Organization.

Contact details

Lawrence Ellyard is happy to receive your feedback, comments and questions. Please note that due to the overwhelming amount of correspondence he receives, he cannot reply personally to all e-mails but makes every attempt to answer questions. He can be reached through his website at: www.lawrenceellyard.com

Or write to Lawrence at: PO Box 548, Fremantle 6959, Western Australia.

Hado websites and related links

Official homepage for Japan's office. IHM Co Ltd: www.hado.com (website in Japanese)

The English official homepage for Japan's office, IHM Co Ltd: www.hado.net

The O Books website, publisher of Lawrence Ellyard's books: www.o-books.net

Love and Thanks to Water Project: www.thank-water.net

I.H.M Hado Life Europe (Liechtenstein): www.hado-life-europe.com (website in German)

Beyond Words Publishing in USA: www.beyondword.com – the publisher of *Hidden Messages in Water* and *The True Power of Water*

The website of *What the bleep do we know?* featuring Masaru Emoto's work: http://whatthebleep.com

Other useful websites:
Al Gore's website on Global Warming: www.climatecrisis.net

ACKNOWLEDGEMENTS

I would first like to acknowledge Masaru Emoto with gratitude from the depths of my being for his vision, willingness and trust to share his research with me. Thanks also to the dedicated team at IHM in Tokyo including: IHM's president Mr Hazaka, Masahiro Someya, Michiko Hayashi, Ayano Furuya, Kimiko Miyazawa, plus Hiro and Jayme Emoto and Dr Peter Slane from Hado Life USA. Thanks goes to Foladé Bell of Elsevier and *Explore* Journal. Thanks go to my editor and to John Hunt from O Books Publishing for your tireless support and for believing in me. Thanks also go to all those who granted endorsements and who remain a constant source of inspiration and reflection in my life. Lastly my love and thanks goes to my beloved wife Marion who is an ocean of patience, love and wisdom.

BIBLIOGRAPHY

H₂O Healing Water for Mind and Body by Anna Selby, Collins and Brown.

The Water Puzzle and the Hexagonal Key by Dr. Mu Shik Jhon.

Hexagonal Water - The Ultimate Solution by MJ Pangman, MSc., Uplifting Press.

Miracle Molecular Structure of Water by Yang Oh and Gil Ho Kim, Dorrance Publishing.

On the Track of Water's Secret by Hans Kronberger and Siegbert Lattacher, Uranus.

The True Power of Water by Masaru Emoto, Atria Books.

Love Thyself – The Message from Water III by Masaru Emoto, Hay House.

The Snowflake, Winter's Secret Beauty by Kenneth Libbrecht, Voyager Press.

Australia's Drinking Water – The Coming Crisis by John Archer, Pure Water Press.

The HeartMath Solution: The Institute of HeartMath's Revolutionary Program for Engaging the Power of the Heart's Intelligence by Doc Lew Childre, Howard Martin Publishers.

Awaken Healing Energy through the Tao by Mantak Chia, Aurora Press.

The Power of Appreciation by Noelle C. Nelson and Jeannine Lemare Calaba, Axiom Publishing.

Web sources

Our special thanks goes to the authors of the following websites for information regarding our research on water.

www.mercola.com/article/distilled_water.htm – Early death comes from drinking distilled water.

http://www.britainexpress.com/Myths/Glastonbury.htm – Glastonbury Legends and Myths. The legend of Joseph of Arimathea at Glastonbury.

http://www.unesco.org/water/wwd2006/world_views/water_religions_beliefs.s

html – UNESCO's website on water and worldviews: *Water, religions and beliefs*.

http://www.bath.ac.uk/~lw235/hexagonal.html – The Mathematics of Honeycomb.

http://www.cnn.com/health/library/fl/00068.html – CNN website, Health library,

http://www.whfoods.com/genpage.php?tname=foodtip&dbid=91 – The George Mateljan Foundation.

http://www.kacha-stones.com/crystal_healing_and_numerology.htm – Crystal Healing & Numbers.

http://www.shirleys-wellness-cafe.com/fluoride.htm – Shirley's Wellness Cafe on Holistic Health: Fluoride.

http://ga.water.usgs.gov/edu/waterproperties.html – USGS website on water science for schools.

http://ga.water.usgs.gov/edu/earthwherewater.html – USGS website on Water science for schools.

http://www.visionlearning.com/library/module_viewer.php?mid=57 – Vision Learning -Water, Properties and Behavior.

http://www.hometrainingtools.com/articles/properties-water-science-teaching-tip.html – home science tools website.

http://www.chem1.com/acad/sci/aboutwater.html – H_2O, a gentle introduction to the structure of water.

http://jersey.uoregon.edu/~mstrick/hydrosphere/Lectures_hydro/Origins_Cycle.html – the origins of water.

http://astrobio.net/news/article1905.html – are we drinking comet water?

http://orthodoxeurope.org/page/12/5.aspx – Russian Orthodox Church representation to the European Institutions.

http://science.nasa.gov/headlines/y2001/ast18may_1.htm – a taste for comet water.

http://www.ifa.hawaii.edu/~hsieh/mbc-release.html – new class of comets may be the source of earth's water.

http://witcombe.sbc.edu/water/physicsuniverse.html – H_2O, the mystery, art and science of water.

http://www.africanwater.org/religion.htm – theWater Page – water in religion.

http://Hado.net/water_crystals1.html – website for Hado International.

http://www.sacredarch.com/sacred_geo_exer_snowflake.htm – the website of Robert A. Armon, architect and artist – The Snowflake Pattern.

http://www.snowcrystals.com - Snow Crystals website.

http://ourworld.compuserve.com/homepages/DP5/pattern1.htm – Patterns in Nature, by David Pratt.

http://www.novareinna.com/constellation/taurusluck.html – the website for Constellation Chamber, Taurus.

http://www.northernearth.co.uk/ftr_eeee.htm – Northern Earth feature, Earth Energies Eclipse Experiment, by Christine Rhone.

http://www.nswscl.org.au/journal/46/Barnett.html – the New South Wales Society for Computers and the Law.

http://hypertextbook.com/facts/2003/ChrisDAmbrose.shtml – the hyper text book website - Frequency Range of Human Hearing.

References

Nature's Miracle – article by Dolly Knight and Jonathan Stromberg Ecovortek's water enhancing treatment technology (W.E.T.)

THE SPIRIT OF WATER - GUIDED MEDITATIONS

Narrated by Lawrence Ellyard

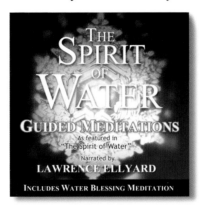

Now you can put the Spirit of Water into action. This CD is ideal for anyone interested in the Power of Water and their Mind.

Track 1. Hado Smile Meditation

A soothing meditation to direct the hado vibration throughout the entire body with the healing power of the smile.

Track 2. Hado Prayer Meditation

An empowering meditation to acknowledge your blessings and to cultivate what you need for your journey throughout life.

Track 3. Self-Love Meditation

A calming meditation to acknowledge and awaken the love, truth and beauty inside you.

Track 4. Love and Gratitude for Self-Healing Meditation

A powerful meditation designed to align your body and mind to the hado of love and gratitude.

Track 5. Love and Gratitude for Healing Others Meditation

A healing meditation designed to subdue pride and cultivate a generous spirit. This meditation directs the hado of healing to those in need.

Track 6. Water Blessing Meditation

A transformative meditation to imbue the vibration of hado into water, cultivating purity and positively charged water.

UK - **£9.99** USA - **$19.95** AUS - **$29.95**
Available at: **http://www.lawrenceellyard.com**

BOOKS

O books
O is a symbol of the world, of oneness and unity. In different cultures it also means the "eye", symbolizing knowledge and insight, and in Old English it means "place of love or home". O books explores the many paths of understanding which different traditions have developed down the ages, particularly those today that express respect for the planet and all of life.

For more information on the full list of over 300 titles please visit our website
www.O-books.net

myspiritradio is an exciting web, internet, podcast and mobile phone global broadcast network for all those interested in teaching and learning in the fields of body, mind, spirit and self development. Listeners can hear the show online via computer or mobile phone, and even download their favourite shows to listen to on MP3 players whilst driving, working, or relaxing.

Feed your mind, change your life with O Books, The O Books radio programme carries interviews with most authors, sharing their wisdom on

mySpiritRadio

life, the universe and everything...e mail questions and co-create the show with O Books and myspiritradio.

Just visit **www.myspiritradio.com** for more information.

OTHER TITLES BY LAWRENCE ELLYARD

Reiki Q&A: 200 Questions & Answers for Beginners

Lawrence Ellyard

2nd printing

This unique handbook clearly answers all kinds of questions about Reiki and its practice as well as dispelling any misconceptions. Useful, dependable and highly recommended. **Penny Parkes**, author of *15-minute Reiki*

1905047479 208pp **£12.99 $24.95**

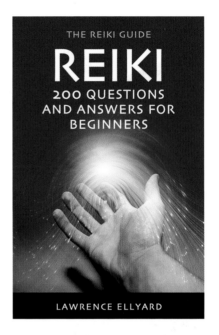

Ultimate Reiki Guide for Practitioners and Masters

Lawrence Ellyard

2nd printing

In this excellent volume, Lawrence Ellyard brings together his considerable expertise and experience to provide a clear and concise view of how to conduct Reiki and to establish oneself as a Reiki practitioner. It will be invaluable for all Reiki professionals and lay persons as a spiritual, practice and business guide. **Dr. Ralph Locke**, CEO, Ikon

1905047487 208pp **£12.99 $24.95**

Everyday Buddha

A contemporary rendering of the

Buddhist classic, the Dhammapada

Karma Yonten Senge (Lawrence Ellyard)

Foreword by **His Holiness the 14th Dalai Lama**

Excellent. Whether you already have a copy of the Dhammapada or not, I recommend you get this. I congratulate all involved in this project and have put the book on my recommended list.

Jeremy Ball Nova Magazine

1905047304 144pp **£9.99 $19.95**